Self-Management and
Cognitive Behavior Interventions

A Tribute to Rich Simpson

Dr. Richard L. Simpson unexpectedly passed away just as this series was about to go to press. He had a significant and profound impact on each of us, the field of special education, and the areas of autism and behavior disorders in particular. Dr. Simpson spent 42 years of his career at the University of Kansas, from where he led the field in developing teacher preparation programs for future educators of students with autism and behavior disorders. He also conducted research to identify scientifically validated practices, and published over 200 articles, books, and book chapters. His work guided the field's effort to bridge the gap between research and practice and advanced the movement to identify and use evidence-based practices that improved the lives of children and youth with autism and their families. Many revered Dr. Simpson. His numerous awards and public recognitions reflect a distinguished career of considerable contribution.

Dr. Simpson was also a remarkable and inspiring teacher and mentor. His knowledge was awe-inspiring, yet he was approachable and personable. He supported graduate students by providing them with many opportunities to publish and conduct research and to complete professional presentations and school-based consultations. His students will carry his legacy throughout the world, working as teachers, school administrators, consultants, researchers, and professors, all serving children and youth with autism and their families.

Those who knew Dr. Simpson will remember his friendly and caring disposition, great sense of humor, and quick wit. He was a wonderful friend to many, and his guidance and encouragement were unparalleled. He will be missed by many, in ways that are too numerous to count.

PRO-ED Series on Autism Spectrum Disorders
Second Edition

Edited by Richard L. Simpson

Titles in the Series

PRO-ED Series on Autism Spectrum Disorders
Second Edition

Self-Management and Cognitive Behavior Interventions

Stephen A. Crutchfield

Leah Wood

8700 Shoal Creek Boulevard
Austin, Texas 78757-6897
800/897-3202   Fax 800/397-7633
www.proedinc.com

© 2018 by PRO-ED, Inc.
8700 Shoal Creek Boulevard
Austin, Texas 78757-6897
800/897-3202   Fax 800/397-7633
www.proedinc.com

Library of Congress Cataloging-in-Publication Data
Self-Management and Cognitive Behavior Interventions
Library of Congress Cataloging-in-Publication Control
Number: 2018016491 (print)

Art Director: Jason Crosier
Designer: Lissa Hattersley
This book is designed in Nexus Serif TF and Formata Sans.

Printed in the United States of America

1 2 3 4 5 6 7 8 9 10   27 26 25 24 23 22 21 20 19 18

Contents

From the Editor

Children and youth with autism spectrum disorder (ASD) routinely demonstrate exceptionally demanding and distinctive characteristics and needs. Even when compared to other disabilities, ASD is especially complex and perplexing. Learners diagnosed with ASD exhibit a range of cognitive, communicative, and social–emotional interests and abilities; and they commonly display a variety of challenging behaviors. Still, many children and adolescents with ASD have normal patterns of growth and development, a wide range of distinctive assets and capabilities, and some individuals with ASD have highly developed and inimitable abilities. These widely varied and unique features necessitate specially designed interventions and strategies orchestrated by knowledgeable and skilled professionals. When supported by the right combination of well-informed professionals (and in many instances parents and family members) and appropriate methods and intervention strategies, children and youth with ASD show significant progress. Without a doubt, consistent and correct use of effective methods, as presented in the current series, is the key to achieving successful outcomes with individuals with ASD.

Preface to the Series

Identification, correct implementation, and ongoing evaluation of scientifically supported and effective practices are essential features of effective programming for learners with ASD. Unquestionably, there is a clear-cut link between use of interventions and supports with empirical backing and positive school and post-school outcomes. Different terms, including *evidence-based procedures and practices*, *scientifically supported interventions*, and *research-validated methods*, all refer to methods and practices that have been successful in bringing about desired changes based on objective and empirically valid research. Unfortunately, practitioners all too often fail to use these proven tools and procedures, or use them the wrong way.

Indeed, this "research-to-practice gap" is a major obstacle in efficiently and effectively addressing the needs of learners with ASD and creating optimal pathways to the best outcomes. This is not a problem of motivation, intent, or objective. Educators and other professionals, as well as parents, families, and other stakeholders, want the most effective methods and updated ASD information. Regrettably, clearly written and practitioner- and family-friendly materials that provide straightforward and user-friendly information and explanations are in short supply.

This concern was the motivation for creating the current resources. Each book in the series provides utilitarian and down-to-earth information on using an intervention or support method with potential to produce significant benefit. Each book, written in a user-friendly and straightforward fashion by experienced internationally recognized professionals, offers practical information, solutions, and strategies for successfully supporting individuals with ASD and related disabilities.

The 9 books in the series offer clear and direct guidance on applying research-supported and proven information, methods, and procedures. The series has the potential to make a significant positive difference for teachers and allied professionals.

Several of the books focus on using applied behavior analysis (ABA), the single most verified intervention tool for learners with ASD. The revised series includes the following:

- de Boer provides step-by-step use of discrete trial instruction and related methodology.
- Tincani, Lorah, and Dowdy direct readers in how to design maximally effective management programs via functional behavior assessment and analysis.

Other skill development foci are covered in the series, each with an emphasis on practical application of documented methods, as evidenced in the following:

- Stichter and Conroy address the ever-pressing issue of building social skill assets among children and youth with ASD and harnessing the support of peers.
- Charlop provides a practitioner-friendly explanation of use of naturalistic teaching strategies and incidental teaching methods.
- Ayres and Whiteside provide essential and utilitarian information on how to take advantage of assistive and instructional-technology tools to teach and support learners with ASD.
- Earles-Vollrath, Cook, and Kemper, in detail, describe efficacious visual supports that can help children and youth with ASD function more effectively and independently.
- Crutchfield and Wood provide readers clear-cut instruction in the use of cognitive behavior modification, self-management, and self-monitoring methods.
- Shogren and Wehmeyer, via their book on self-determination, offer specific and clearly described strategies for ensuring individuals with ASD are fully and deservedly involved in their program plans and outcomes.
- Finally, Travers addresses the all-too-often-neglected topic of sexuality matters among adolescents and young adults with autism-related disabilities.

Richard L. Simpson
Series Editor

Acknowledgments

We would like to thank all of the classroom teachers and curriculum specialists who contributed to this work by sending us examples of self-management and cognitive behavioral strategies. The work you do daily for students with autism makes this work possible and more meaningful.

Thank you!

Sabrina Mitchell, PhD – Autism/Behavioral Specialist, Lee's Summit R-7, Lee's Summit, MO

Angela Chamber, MS – Classroom Teacher, Lee's Summit R-7 School District, Lee's Summit, MO

Sarah Weber, MS, BCBA – Classroom Teacher, The Joshua School, Denver, CO

Melissa Pace-Spivey, MA – Classroom Teacher, Atascadero Unified School District, Atascadero, CA

April Haworth, MA – Classroom Teacher, Atascadero Unified School District, Atascadero, CA

Kate Anderson, MA – Classroom Teacher, San Luis Coastal School District, Los Osos, CA

Logan Duarte, MA – Classroom Teacher, Lucia Mar Unified School District, Arroyo Grande, CA

Leah Payne, MA – Classroom Teacher, Guadalupe Union School District, Guadalupe, CA

Elena Jaquez, MA – Classroom Teacher, Santa Maria Bonita School District, Santa Maria, CA

Erin Fisher, MA – Graduate Student, California Polytechnic State University, San Luis Obispo, CA

Adam Dale, MA – Classroom Teacher, San Luis Coastal Unified School District, San Luis Obispo, CA

Ashleigh Brendlen, MA – Classroom Teacher, Union School District, San Jose, CA

Figures 1.5, 1.6, 1.11, 1.12, 1.15, 1.16, 1.17, 2.1, 2.3, and 2.5 all use one or more symbols with permission from Mayer-Johnson:

Mayer-Johnson LLC. (2015). *Picture communication symbols*. Available from www.mayer-johnson.com or Tobii Dynavox at 2100 Wharton Street, #400, Pittsburgh, PA 15203. Phone 1(800) 588-4548, fax 1(866) 585-6260, or e-mail mayer-johnson.usa@mayer-johnson.com.

Introduction

Before we begin to unpack self-management and cognitive behavior intervention strategies for students with autism spectrum disorder (ASD), it is very important that we define certain terms and come to a shared understanding of several of the theoretical underpinnings of the interventions discussed in this guide. The first concept to unpack is cognitive behavior modification (CBM). *Cognitive behavior modification* is an umbrella term that refers to a variety of programs and treatments that rely on both cognitive processes (e.g., self-evaluation, problem solving) and behavioral approaches (e.g., positive reinforcement, priming, modeling) to ultimately change behavior. These approaches are notoriously broad and somewhat disconnected, but at their heart these treatments attempt to shift the responsibility for behavior change or skill production to the target individual (Maag, 1989). In this way, these approaches seek to increase an individual's self-management. Broadly defined, *self-management* is synonymous with self-regulation or self-control, and it refers to the cognitive processes that allow one to voluntarily control one's own emotional and behavioral responses (Blair & Diamond, 2008). Self-management encompasses a wide variety of cognitive (or thinking) processes, which include but are not limited to controlling emotions, attending to relevant information, planning future behavior, remaining flexible through unplanned setbacks, and behaving in a way that enhances the likelihood of achieving future goals (Blair & Diamond, 2008). Importantly, successful self-management is one of the ultimate goals of most educational programs.

It is well documented that individuals with ASD often demonstrate deficits in key areas of self-management (see Adrien et al., 1995; Ozonoff & McEvoy, 1994). Because of these deficits, individuals with ASD are often overwhelmed by intense emotions, may be unable to plan ahead, may lack flexibility in thinking and action, may perform poorly in social interactions, and may lack other goal-directed behaviors (Jahromi, Bryce, & Swanson, 2013; Loveland, 2005). These deficits can negatively impact all areas of life for individuals with ASD, from social relationships and school success to postsecondary job opportunities and overall quality of life. Further confounding these difficulties, some individuals with ASD are likely to develop mood disorders (e.g., anxiety, depression) and demonstrate symptoms of conduct disorder or anger management issues because of poorly developed self-management (Kim, Szatmari, Bryson, Streiner, & Wilson, 2000). Thankfully, there are specific strategies that have proved effective in supporting specific self-management processes for students with ASD. In this book we examine specific, efficacious self-management interventions and cognitive behavioral interventions for students with ASD.

Self-management interventions (SMIs) are a specific type of CBM. These approaches are specific interventions that are managed by the target individual and are used to address a wide variety of targeted outcomes. Traditionally, school-based treatments for individuals with ASD have been notoriously teacher managed, meaning that many of the approaches we use to improve outcomes for students with ASD are largely developed, implemented, and managed by the teacher or other school support personnel (Wilkinson, 2008). Such interventions as video modeling, explicit and systematic instruction, and visual supports are largely teacher-managed tools. Attempts to fade use of these teacher-managed approaches or eventually train students to use them independently often fail without the direct support of teachers. In contrast, SMIs are approaches that are developed by teachers and other practitioners but are ultimately, to various degrees, implemented and managed by the target individual. Examples of SMIs include, but are not limited to, goal setting, self-monitoring, self-evaluation, self-instruction, positive self-talk, self-reinforcement, and other metacognitive approaches (Quinn, Swaggart, & Myles, 1994). When implemented appropriately, SMI can help students become more self-managed and in control of their own behavior.

Besides SMIs, there are other CBM approaches that have proved useful for students with ASD. These *cognitive behavioral interventions* (CBIs) encompass approaches designed to help individuals examine their thoughts and emotions, recognize when their emotions are running high or when they are engaging in "bad thinking," and adopt actions that change their thinking and ultimately their behavior (Scarpa, White, & Attwood, 2013). These curricula commonly address social deficits and are often packaged with behavioral principles, such as positive reinforcement, modeling, and immediate feedback in order to bring about the desired behavior change or skill acquisition. To further illustrate these interrelated concepts, let us briefly explore a real-life example that illuminates the importance of these tools in everyday life.

Suppose you are running late to a very important meeting. Traffic is surprisingly congested as you make your way through the city, and with each passing minute you realize you are not going to make the agreed-upon meeting time. You decide to call ahead and alert the other stakeholders of your predicament. Unfortunately, you are unable to get a reliable cell signal and the call will not go through. As you plod along, your mind conjures an image of your colleagues sitting around a table waiting for you to arrive, and you grow more frustrated by your absence with each passing moment. You begin to feel helpless and increasingly angry as the traffic inches down the freeway. Another motorist, perhaps experiencing a similar delay, attempts to rapidly switch lanes, and in so doing, cuts you off. You slam on your brakes to keep from crashing into the other car and consequently spill your steaming cup of coffee on your lap and the newly cleaned console of your vehicle. In that moment, you lose control of yourself and begin to act in a way that does not support your desired outcome (arriving at work on time). You lay on your horn, scream your favorite swear words, and generally feel overwhelmed by the intensity of your emotions. This momentary loss of self-control could have disastrous consequences: You could endanger others on the road by driving more aggressively, you could get in a fender bender and further prevent yourself from arriving at your meeting, or the feelings of frustration and anxiety could render you ineffective when you do arrive at work.

We can all relate to this example because we have all had similar lapses in self-control. Thankfully, for most people, these lapses are few and far between. To combat these lapses, we often employ certain tools to improve our self-control capabilities and ensure that these lapses remain infrequent. For example, you might employ a specific SMI to avoid this loss of control in the future. To do this, you might set a goal to leave the house earlier each morning (goal setting). To monitor your progress on this goal, you might record the time you get in your car each morning to depart for work (self-monitoring). Further, you might reward yourself with your favorite cocktail or dessert when you meet this goal for an entire week (self-reinforcement). These approaches represent specific self-management procedures that you have adopted to improve your overall well-being and functioning. You might do these things instinctively without even recognizing that you are managing yourself. Other people might examine their feelings whenever they become agitated, recognize that these feelings impair their ability to make good decisions, and take actions to calm their emotional responses. To do this they may engage in a specific CBI, such as positive self-talk, or in specific coping procedures, such as listening to their favorite song to feel calm. Regardless, these approaches allow us to regain control of ourselves and return to behaving in a way that will better serve our short-term and long-term goals.

Certainly, these lapses in self-management occur more frequently for certain individuals, and as discussed, many individuals with ASD have poorly developed self-management techniques. Thankfully, there are specific research-based strategies for supporting specific self-management processes for students with ASD. In this book, we focus on some of these specific approaches. First, in Part One of this guide, we examine self-management interventions and explore how these interventions can be designed and implemented for students with ASD. Of all the CBM approaches, SMIs have the most empirical support and are widely used in educational settings for students with ASD. In Part Two of this guide, we provide overviews of specific cognitive behavior interventions. While many specific practices and strategies fall under the broad umbrella of CBI, it is our goal in Part Two to highlight the most effective and useful of these approaches and provide practitioners and parents with clear guidelines and recommendations.

PART ONE Self-Management Interventions

What Are Self-Management Interventions?

As discussed in the introduction, self-management interventions (SMIs) assist individuals in directing their own behavior to achieve specific goals (Yeung & Yeung, 2016). Successfully engaging in self-management requires an individual to actively monitor his or her own thinking, emotions, and actions and make the adjustments needed to meet personal short-term and long-term goals (Barlow, Wright, Sheasby, Turner, & Hainsworth, 2002). SMIs are used in a variety of spaces outside of education, including medicine (Muchmore, Springer, & Miller, 1994), mental health (Ben-Zeev et al., 2013), exercise sciences (Nicklas et al., 2014), and self-help (Burke, Wang, & Sevick, 2011), and these strategies have contributed to quality of life improvements for people from all walks of life. In fact, you can probably think of SMIs that you use on a daily or weekly basis. Perhaps you set certain financial or exercise goals and use monitoring systems to track your spending or physical activities.

SMIs and Students With ASD

For students with autism spectrum disorder (ASD), SMIs have proved effective for a variety of learning outcomes. The National Center for Professional Development on Autism Spectrum Disorders (NCPD-ASD), a multi-university center for developing and promoting evidence-based practices (EBPs) for students with autism funded by the Office of Special Education Programs (OSEP), and the National Autism Standards Project both list SMIs as an EBP for school-age students with ASD. Further, SMIs may be particularly useful in school settings given that they can be maintained without the direct supervision of and implementation by an instructor and are often dynamic systems that are adaptable to the specific needs of the student and the environment (Koegel & Koegel, 1990; Lee, Simpson, & Shogren, 2007). Finally, self-management skills have been identified as pivotal skills for students with ASD, indicating that when students learn to manage their own behavioral outcomes, improvements are seen in a variety of untargeted behaviors and environments (Koegel, Koegel, & McNerney, 2001).

Types of SMIs

There are several types of SMIs, including (but not limited to) goal setting, self-evaluation, self-instruction, self-assessment, self-monitoring, and self-reinforcement (Davis, Mason, Davis, Mason, & Crutchfield, 2016). While these types of interventions have some utility for students with ASD, it is not feasible to provide implementation guidelines for each of these SMIs in this guide. Rather, we focus on the most common types of SMIs for individuals with ASD. Specifically, this guide focuses on goal-setting interventions, self-monitoring interventions, and self-reinforcement (see Table 1.1 for a brief definition of each of these interventions). It is our opinion that these interventions should be used together as a package treatment for students with ASD, when appropriate. We feel strongly that combining these approaches can lead to better outcomes and greater independence for students with ASD, while having the biggest impact on the desired skills. However, we also realize that some students may not benefit from one or more of these approaches, and thus it is our goal to present each of these SMIs with sufficient detail to allow for their use as a stand-alone intervention.

What Types of Students With ASD Benefit From SMIs?

SMIs have demonstrated broad effectiveness for many students in school settings, including students who are typically developing; students with learning disabilities, attention deficits, or cognitive impairments; and students with autism. Specifically, for students with ASD, self-management has also demonstrated broad effectiveness, with positive results reported for students across the autism spectrum (Crutchfield, Mason, Chambers, Wills, & Mason, 2016). Similarly, research supports the use of self-monitoring for both elementary and secondary students

Table 1.1. Brief Definitions of SMIs Covered in This Guide

Intervention	Definition
Goal setting	Involves the identification and recording of specific short-term or long-term goals by the individual
Self-monitoring	Involves the collection and recording of specific data features (frequency, duration, etc.) over time by the individual
Self-reinforcement	Involves the self-evaluation of goal/criteria attainment and the self-administration of desired stimuli

with ASD. This is not to suggest that *all* students with ASD will benefit from all SMIs. Clearly, we should make every attempt to align the features of this evidence-based practice with the specific characteristics of the target student. Toward this goal, we have included information on specific prerequisite skills that teachers will need to consider when planning the specific SMIs discussed in this guide.

Further, while self-management strategies have a good deal of evidence supporting their use for students with ASD, they will likely not be effective in environments that are not conducive to best practices. For example, even well-designed SMI programs applied in unstructured and disorganized classrooms will likely result in poor outcomes. Similarly, if they are developed without considering the unique characteristics and preferences of individual students, then we cannot expect these programs to effectively change behavior. The self-management systems that will be most effective and efficient are those that are (a) developed within a larger framework of best practices (e.g., including well-trained and caring staff, engaging and universally designed materials, sound instructional approaches, data-based decision making) and (b) individualized according to a student's needs and preferences (Simpson & Crutchfield, 2013). Figure 1.1 outlines these considerations relative to self-management.

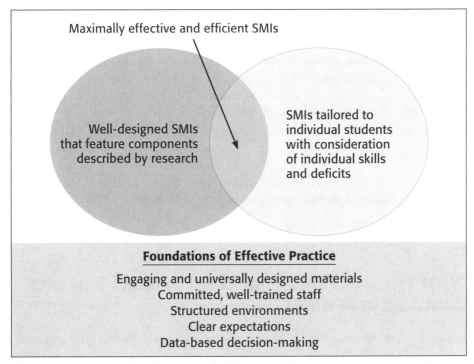

Figure 1.1. Maximally effective and efficient self-management interventions (SMIs).

We begin this guide by discussing specific SMIs, including goal setting, self-monitoring, and self-reinforcement, and present clear guidelines on implementing these interventions. We complete the SMI section of this manual by providing a case study that illustrates the use of these approaches in concert, that is, as a packaged self-management treatment for students with ASD.

What Are Goal-Setting Interventions?

Goal-setting interventions include teaching students to identify measurable targets and to develop plans for accomplishing the targets (Sands & Doll, 2000). Goal-setting interventions are a natural starting point for SMIs, as goal-directed behavior is necessary for the other components of these treatments. Goal setting is salient to self-management because it fixes a future target to which we can compare current performance. Without goal setting, self-monitoring is pointless and self-reinforcement is arbitrary. We certainly recognize the importance of setting goals for students in special education, as this activity is the foundation of the Individualized Education Program (IEP). However, in our field, we sometimes overlook the value in supporting students in *setting their own goals*. Students who set their own goals are more likely to be aware of their learning outcomes and more engaged in the process of attaining them. Further, as students with special needs progress through their programs, they are (or should be) expected to participate in the development of their own IEP and eventually lead or participate in discussions about their own strengths, weaknesses, and future goals and desires. It is unlikely that many students with ASD will be able to accomplish this without specific instruction and scaffolds in goal-setting procedures. Because of these factors, and the general self-management skills (including goal-directed behavior) that students with ASD so often lack, improving the goal-setting capabilities of these students is a worthwhile endeavor. It is important to note that goal-setting approaches are most often developed for students with ASD as part of a larger self-management plan (see Shogren & Wehmeyer's *Self-Determination* book in this series). Toward this end, we describe goal-setting interventions as the initiating activity of a larger self-management intervention.

What Types of Goals Should We Support Students With ASD in Setting?

When supporting students with ASD in developing their own goals, we should consider the *length* of the goal and the *attainability* of the goal. Typically, goals are described as long term or short term. In school, long-term goals may be annual

IEP goals or school-wide goals, like reading 1 million words in a year or meeting Accelerated Reader quarterly goals. Outside of school, long-term goals might include obtaining a job, completing college, or finding a romantic partner. School-based, short-term goals might include goals that can be more quickly attained and may include the completion of discrete steps that lead toward a long-term goal. For example, a short-term goal might be reading 1,000 words, talking to a friend on the playground, or completing homework every day for 2 weeks. Outside of school, short-term goals might include cleaning one's apartment, riding the bus to work independently, or completing five job applications. It is good to teach students about the different temporal characteristics of goals, and students with ASD may benefit from guided discussions that help them consider and develop personally relevant long-term goals, particularly as their interests and goals may help drive short-term goal development. Ultimately, steering students toward the selection and development of short-term goals will help them choose targets that can be completed in a short amount of time, and therefore they will be reinforced more frequently.

Another feature of goals to teach students is the appropriateness or attainability of a goal. This means we may have to shape student goal-setting behavior and help learners select goals that are realistic and can be readily achieved in a school environment. For example, a student who selects the regrettably unattainable goal of *being* Batman may need help in identifying characteristics or traits of Batman that he or she can work toward. Maybe instead, an attainable but related goal is to show Batman-like strength by being a leader during transitions. Another way teachers can shape an understanding of attainable or realistic goal selection is by controlling the goals students may select. Teachers may initially provide an array of choices of goals that have been prewritten by the teacher. While these goals should still align with student strengths, needs, and interests, they can be better managed by being attainable, short-term choices. Again, by shaping students' behaviors and providing guidance, teachers can still engage students in meaningful goal-setting behaviors that may increase engagement in school-based activities and motivation to persist and succeed.

A final feature of student goals is that they address behaviors the student has already mastered. Self-selecting and self-monitoring goals is almost never an appropriate approach for novel skills. Teachers still must develop and provide formal plans of study, based on IEP goals and grade-aligned state standards. Goals best suited for student-driven goal-setting interventions should be based on behaviors the student has already learned but needs to fine-tune. For example, learning to read (as a novel skill) would not be a good goal for a student to self-select, but reading one chapter of a book would be appropriate (for a student who has already learned how to read). This does not mean that we would discourage students from recognizing and voicing long-term goals or desires to learn new skills. However, when helping students develop targeted and attainable goals for goal-setting interventions, we should steer students toward goals that will yield a high rate of success. We want them to select goals they can easily learn to define, monitor, and achieve, so that their behaviors will be reinforced (both their target behavior and the process of setting and monitoring goals). Ultimately, we are teaching students a self-management process by helping them select goals that they are likely able to meet.

Goal-setting interventions should address four different skills (Lee, Palmer, & Wehmeyer, 2009):

1. Set meaningful, measurable goals.
2. Develop a plan to achieve the goals.
3. Develop a system for measuring progress toward the goals.
4. Establish consequences for goal achievement.

The following section describes specific strategies for teaching students with ASD to accomplish each of the steps for setting and achieving goals.

What Prerequisite Skills Do Students With ASD Need for Goal-Setting Interventions?

To benefit from goal-setting interventions, students with ASD should be able to

- provide information about personal strengths, needs, and interests;
- choose from an array of preselected choices or goals; and
- demonstrate understanding of the concept of *most* (i.e., order choices by personal relevance or importance).

These prerequisite skills align with the tools students will need to make meaningful selections about their own areas of need (as opposed to prerequisite skills related to developing goals based on any whim, interest, or preference). Therefore, we recommend students have the ability to think critically about appropriate goal selections in order to benefit from goal-setting interventions. Students who are unable to demonstrate these skills can certainly be systematically taught to engage in these behaviors (the steps to teach these behaviors are outlined in the pages of this guide), and it is our belief that even students with ASD and cognitive impairments can benefit from goal-setting interventions. However, like all evidence-based-practice implementation, selecting students who are likely to benefit from the prescribed treatment will lead to the most effective and efficient results.

Steps in Implementing Goal-Setting Interventions

The four main steps in setting goals are

1. selecting and defining a goal,
2. developing a plan for achieving the goal,
3. developing a measurement system for monitoring progress toward achievement of the goal, and
4. establishing consequences.

The process of setting goals can be very abstract and even initially overwhelming to students. Thus a good approach to use across the steps is a gradual release of responsibility model of instruction (Pearson & Gallagher, 1983). This model is very common in special education and describes the explicit instruction format of a model–lead–test approach to teaching. The goal is always to systematically fade teacher support over time and transfer responsibility to the student, but this transfer should occur only when students are demonstrating readiness and understanding. By controlling and modeling the selection and development of goals initially, teachers can help students develop an understanding of how to select and develop personal goals. Each step of the goal-setting process will include this teacher-driven to student-driven approach. As mentioned previously, the purpose of goal-setting interventions is for students to set or select personally relevant goals in order to increase engagement and motivation to learn and persist. Whether students are choosing from a preselected array of short-term, attainable goals or evaluating their personal strengths and interests to develop their own goals, the overarching purpose remains the same. For students with ASD to benefit from goal-setting interventions, instruction will most likely begin with a good deal of modeling, shaping, and prompting from a teacher. Over time, and based on student needs and characteristics, these supports can be systematically faded. Let us now discuss each step in turn.

Step 1: Selecting and Defining a Goal

To select a meaningful goal, students should first self-assess their own strengths, needs, and interests (Shogren, Wehmeyer, Burke, & Palmer, 2017). Students with ASD may benefit from explicit, guided instruction on how to consider one's own personal characteristics. A graphic organizer and explicit teacher modeling may help students classify strengths, needs, and interests. Students with high-functioning autism spectrum disorder (HFASD) may be able to complete this task with the support of initial teacher modeling and a worksheet with guiding questions or sentence stems (e.g., "My strengths are _____; I need help with _____; I am interested in ____"). For example, an initial lesson in which a teacher uses think-aloud modeling to demonstrate how he or she considers personal strengths, needs, and interests may be enough instruction for students to engage in their own personal reflection. Students with more extensive support needs might benefit from first learning the concepts of a strength, a need, and an interest. Teachers can use constant time delay procedures to teach recognition of these terms, if the terms themselves are not in the student's repertoire (i.e., first ask the student to name or point to each term while simultaneously naming or pointing to the target term for the student; in the next round of instruction, ask the student to name or point to each term, but wait 4 seconds before providing the correct response). Then, it may be necessary to also teach the concept of each term. A good research-based approach for teaching concepts is example/nonexample training (or discrimination training). This explicit instruction technique helps students differentiate between key features of distinct categories or classes of information. For example, teachers can present word or picture cards that are examples and nonexamples of personal strengths and then use model–lead–test procedures to teach students to discriminate between examples and nonexamples of each term. After this pretraining, students with more extensive support needs are ready to make a personal selection of strengths, needs, and interests. The specific response options can (and should) be controlled by the teacher to include known areas of strengths, needs, and interests for individual students, as well as distractors (nonexamples). Examples of self-reflection inventories for students who have HFASD or who require more extensive supports are shown in Figure 1.2. This inventory is an example of Part A of a goal-setting worksheet.

Next, students should use knowledge of self to choose or develop one goal. Goals can range in foci and can vary based on students' individual learner characteristics. Examples of goal categories include (but are not limited to) *academic goals* (e.g., academic readiness, grade-aligned goals, goals related to IEP goals), *organizational goals* (e.g., completing work tasks, submitting work on time), or *social interactions* (e.g., engaging in conversations with peers, participating in group activities during recess or breaks). For some students, teachers may need to teach the concept of distinct categories of goals, using example/nonexample training. Using a gradual release of responsibility approach, teachers can begin by guiding students to select a predetermined category of goals. For example, using known information about the student (e.g., the student has difficulty completing work on time and the student is interested in learning about outer space), teachers can help shape the selection of student goals that are both appropriate and based on student input. Students with ASD may also benefit from a decision-making tool when selecting or choosing an initial goal. This process can help students see the

---

Example for students with HFASD

Goal-Setting Worksheet

Part A: Thinking about myself

1. My strengths are: _____
_____
_____

2. I need help with: _____
_____
_____

3. I am interested in: _____
_____
_____

Example for students with more extensive support needs

Goal-Setting Worksheet

Part A: Thinking about myself

1. My strengths are:

| reading | math | talking with friends | finishing my work |

2. I need help with:

| reading | math | talking with friends | finishing my work |

3. I am interested in:

| firemen | cars | playing with others | computer time |

Figure 1.2. Example of Part A of a goal-setting worksheet. The example for students with HFASD shows a strengths, needs, and interests inventory. The example for students with more extensive support needs provides preselected, personalized response options.

connection between their own identification of strengths, needs, and interests and a possible goal. Even if teachers have preselected appropriate goal categories, they can help students see the relatedness of their own needs and types of goals. Students with HFASD may benefit from a decision tree that leads them through the process of comparing self-reflection responses to categories of goals, seeking teacher input, and prioritizing possible goals. Even if teachers provide a good deal of guidance about the type of goal, or limit categories so students must select from an array of possible goals, students will benefit from considering the relatedness of their personal strengths, needs, and interests and personal goals. Students with ASD with more extensive support needs may benefit from sentence stems with picture supports and predetermined categories or choices. See Figure 1.3 for an example of Part B of a goal-setting worksheet.

Several key features of this decision-making tool may contribute to a student's understanding of what it means to select a personal goal. For students with HFASD, the questions embedded in the flowchart encourage students to consider the importance of personal strengths, needs, and interests. For students with more extensive support needs, picture supports may help increase understanding of the underlying concepts (e.g., academic learning, social interactions). Instructional approaches focused on systematically teaching students to use the decision tree or sentence stems can also support understanding. For example, teachers can use think-aloud modeling to demonstrate how to use this portion of the worksheet and how to consider personally relevant responses for each question. For students with autism, these supports may provide the structure needed to understand a concrete process for an abstract concept.

Some students with ASD may need additional supports to fully understand the concepts of the categories themselves. A preteaching exercise that discusses the concept of categories, such as *academics, organization skills*, and *social skills*, may be necessary for increased understanding of the tasks. By providing multiple examples of academic goals versus *not* academic goals, teachers can help students understand the meaning of the broad categories from the decision tree. For a sample script of example/nonexample training of goal types, see Table 1.2.

After considering areas of need across categories, students must evaluate the areas of need and select one area to prioritize. For some students, think-aloud modeling of this thought process may be enough to provide understanding of the task demand. For other students with more extensive support needs, it may benefit them to receive pretraining on the concept of *most*. For example, students may need to practice prioritizing three things according to what they need or want "the most." This pretraining exercise will help ensure that (a) students are selecting a topic for a goal that has personal meaning and (b) students recognize that the goal addresses a true area of need. The key to this step of the goal-setting process is that teachers help students select a topic that relates to an area

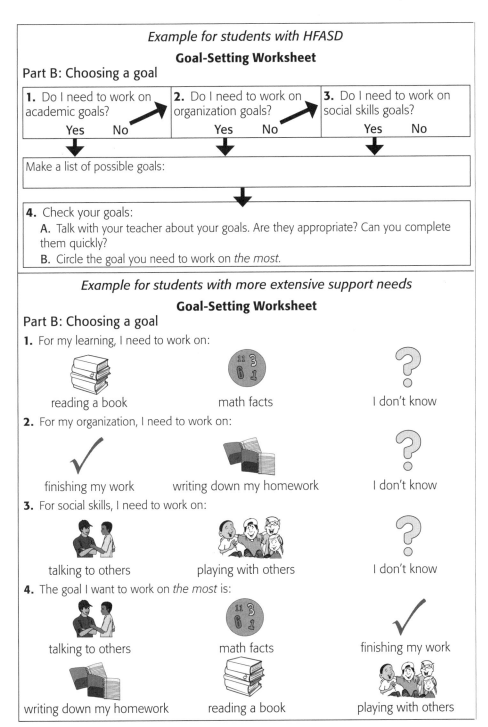

Figure 1.3. Example of Part B of a goal-setting worksheet. The example for students with HFASD shows a decision tree. The example for students with more extensive support needs provides preselected, personalized response options.

Table 1.2. Sample Script of Example/Nonexample Training
of Goal Categories

	Teacher says/does	Student says/does
Model	Starting with the concept of academic, place 5–7 related concept cards in a line on the table. Say, "Let's talk about what 'academic' means." Verbally label each card as "academic" or "not academic" by stating a key feature that identifies the card as an example or nonexample. Model holding up a green check mark or a red X response card for a visual cue for each example or nonexample.	Watches and listens to the teacher.
Lead	Reorder the cards. Say, "Now let's say these together. Help me decide if each card shows 'academic' or 'not academic.' We can use our response cards to show what we think." Guide the student to correctly label each card by saying and/or showing the appropriate response. Provide error correction and specific praise as needed.	Says and/or shows "academic" or "not academic" with the teacher.
Test	Reorder the cards. Say, "Now you get to show me all by yourself. You can tell me or show me what you think." Provide error correction and specific praise as needed.	Says and/or shows "academic" or "not academic" independently.

of need or a personal interest. As mentioned earlier, training this step may require a gradual release of responsibility over an extended period of time, wherein the teacher initially provides more guidance and support in the selection of the focus of the goal. Over time, teachers should gradually and systematically fade that support and provide fewer direct suggestions to promote increased student independence.

After students select a personally relevant focus for the goal, teachers can help them define the goal. Key features of goals are their length and scope. For example, regarding length, teachers can help students consider the duration of the goal. Standard practice in education is for teachers to set both long-term and short-term goals. When developing IEP goals, we consider a year's progress and sometimes break the annual goal into periodic benchmarks. When teaching, we often set weekly, biweekly, or quarterly goals. A standard in short-term goal setting is 2-week time periods. Two weeks is often a reasonable amount of time in which a student can make discernable progress toward a specific goal. Typically, teachers are trained to monitor progress across 2-week segments and then analyze the data at the end of that time. Teachers can make instructional decisions about the adequacy of progress or diagnose difficulties with learner motivation within this period. Two weeks is generally long enough to see progress in graphed data and short enough to make instructional changes in a timely manner as needed. While we do not have to always encourage or teach students to set their own goals in 2-week increments, this is a reasonable amount of time for many goals. Helping students select shorter goals is also a way to build capacity toward completion of a long-term goal. For example, for the long-term goal example provided earlier of "reading 1 million words across a school year," a series of short-term goals of reading 1,000 words per week may help students focus on smaller, attainable benchmarks that can build progress toward the ultimate goal.

Another consideration for the length of goals is that it is important that students be reinforced for accomplishing goals often enough to ensure they value the payoff of their goal-setting behaviors. For example, if students are taught to set or choose only long-term goals, they may lose interest or motivation to complete the goals over time. If students are initially taught to set or choose goals that can be accomplished quickly, they are more likely to be reinforced (both extrinsically and intrinsically) more frequently, increasing the likelihood that their goal-setting behavior will maintain in the future.

Regarding scope, teachers can help students determine a reasonable accomplishment within the predetermined length of the goal. For example, how many vocabulary words does the student want to learn in a 2-week unit on ecosystems? How many books does the student want to read this week? How many peers does the student want to engage in conversation today during free period? To teach students to set appropriate lengths and scopes, teachers can use strategies similar to teaching students to select a goal topic. First, teachers may have to provide more modeling initially, and they may have to provide more guidance to help the students select reasonable lengths and scopes. It is reasonable (and recommended, especially for initial instruction) for teachers to provide a lot of parameters and guidance around both the scope and length of the target goal. That is, the purpose is not for students to have carte blanche to control all aspects of their goal at all times. But teaching students about the concepts of scope and length of goals may be a way to promote generalization of goal-setting behaviors across time and contexts. Over time, teachers should plan to systematically release or withdraw this support and promote greater student independence. A goal-setting worksheet can help students consider and understand the length and scope of the goal, even if goal parameters of scope and length have been preestablished by the teacher. By being provided with sentence stems and think-aloud modeling, students with ASD, especially those with HFASD, can learn the processes necessary for selecting and defining reasonable goals. Students with more extensive support needs may benefit from additional picture supports and preselected response options. See Figure 1.4 for Part C of a goal-setting worksheet.

Some students with ASD may require additional supports to complete Step 1. Students who need communication supports may benefit from technology supports. Apps like GoWorksheet Maker or Kidspiration allow teachers to create worksheets or graphic organizers with supported text features. For instance, a supported technological version of the decision tree might include an option for students to touch and listen to response options before making a final selection. Students may drag and drop response options to complete sentences and then voice their goals using text-to-speech features. For students who have difficulty producing written text, technology can allow them to record a response on the graphic organizer instead of writing a response. See Figure 1.5 for an example of a goal-setting worksheet with embedded technology supports.

Step 2: Developing a Plan for Achieving the Goal

Once students have selected a target goal and set parameters, it is time for teachers to help them create an action plan (Lee et al., 2009). Key features of developing a plan include identifying the necessary steps for achieving the goal (what will the student do?) and barriers that need to be addressed or removed in order for the student to enact the plan (Shogren et al., 2017). Not all goals will require step-by-step plans, and as mentioned earlier, the types of goals students select (or we preselect for students as goal choices) should be goals already in the students' repertoire. Goal-setting interventions are *not* for teaching novel skills, but rather they are for helping students fine-tune or improve behaviors they already know how to do. Still, to ensure that students think carefully about how to successfully accomplish their goal and to ensure that students with cognitive support needs can accomplish their goal, careful planning is required and is an important component of goal-setting interventions. Some goals will be very straightforward, while others may require step-by-step procedures or further consideration. This section describes methods for teaching students to consider all the components necessary for successful achievement of the target goal.

When necessary, teaching students to identify the steps needed for achieving a goal can start with backward planning. We can teach students to consider their end goal using think-aloud modeling (e.g., a teacher might say, "My goal is to read two books in 2 weeks. This means that by the end of 2 weeks, I want to be finished reading two books that I pick out, and I want to learn something from the books I read"). Specific steps for developing a plan can include (a) identifying

(text continues on p. 18)

Example for students with HFASD

Goal-Setting Worksheet

Part C: Choosing the scope and length of my goal

1. My goal topic is: _____

2. For this goal, I will learn or do this much, or this often: _____

_____

3. I need this long to achieve my goal: _____

_____

4. Here is my final goal:

I will (*topic and scope*)_____

and I will be finished in (*length of time to complete my goal*) _____

_____

Example for students with more extensive support needs

Goal-Setting Worksheet

Part C: Choosing scope and length of my goal

1. My topic is:

reading   math   talking to others   finishing my work

2. I will finish (scope):

all   some   none

3. I need this much time to be finished with my goal (length):

(a)   1   2   3   4   5

Monday
22

Monday	Tuesday	Wednesday	Thursday	Friday
22	23	24	25	26

(b)   days   weeks

Figure 1.4. Example of Part C of a goal-setting worksheet. The example for students with HFASD presents sentence stems for determining the scope and length of the goal. The example for students with more extensive support needs provides preselected, personalized response options. The wording and response options will vary based on the goal topics.

_____'s Goal-Setting Worksheet

Part A: Thinking about myself

1. My strengths are:

reading   math   talking with others   finishing my work

2. I need help with:

reading   math   talking with others   finishing my work

3. I am interested in:

firemen   cars   playing with others   computer time

Part B: Choosing a *focus* for my goal

1. For my learning, I need to work on:

reading a book   math facts   I don't know

2. For my organization, I need to work on:

finishing my work   writing down my homework   I don't know

Figure 1.5. Example of a complete goal-setting worksheet (Parts A–C) for students with ASD who have extensive support needs and benefit from technology. A similar version of this worksheet can be created using GoWorksheet Maker, an iOS app from Attainment Company (2017). Features include text-to-speech capabilities for headings and directions (accessed by touching the blue-and-white audio icons), easy responding (circling choices with a finger or stylus), text-to-speech capabilities to voice all response options as needed (see the grey box around the word and image of *all* in Part C for an example of a response option that has been tapped in order to voice the word *all*), and the option to record either an audio response or a typed response in the goal box at the end of Part C. These same supports could be applied to a version of the worksheet for students with HFASD, as needed.

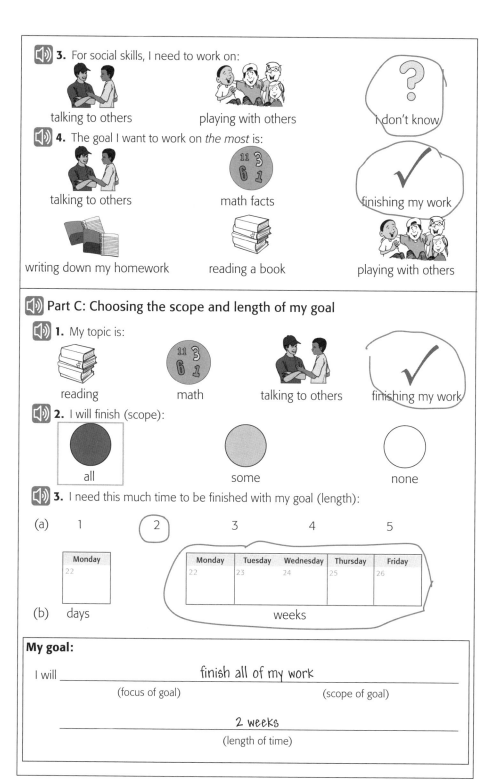

3. For social skills, I need to work on:

talking to others   playing with others   I don't know

4. The goal I want to work on *the most* is:

talking to others   math facts   finishing my work

writing down my homework   reading a book   playing with others

Part C: Choosing the scope and length of my goal

1. My topic is:

reading   math   talking to others   finishing my work

2. I will finish (scope):

all   some   none

3. I need this much time to be finished with my goal (length):

(a)   1   2   3   4   5

Monday
22

Monday	Tuesday	Wednesday	Thursday	Friday
22	23	24	25	26

(b)   days   weeks

My goal:

I will _____ finish all of my work _____

(focus of goal)   (scope of goal)

_____ 2 weeks _____

(length of time)

Figure 1.5. (*continued*)

the materials students will need to reach their goal, (b) identifying the steps students will need to take to reach that goal, (c) identifying any barriers or challenges students need to consider, and (d) selecting strategies for eliminating barriers.

First, teach students to identify materials or supplies they may need to accomplish the goal. For example, students may need books to read. Some students may benefit from a bank of choices. Some choices can include distractor items (items they do *not* need to accomplish their goal). The teacher can model making selections by considering whether each item is relevant or not relevant to the goal. For example, using think-aloud modeling, a teacher could model how to select books (for a goal about reading books) from an array of movies, books, math manipulatives, or calculators. Students with ASD with less extensive support needs may benefit from a simple planning sheet or graphic organizer that prompts them to consider key features of the materials they need. For the example about reading, this could include matters like the length or reading level of the book and the topic of the book (*Is the book interesting to me? Is this a book other kids my age are reading?*). Figure 1.6 provides an example of Part A of a goal-planning worksheet.

Next, if needed and if applicable, teach students to identify the steps they will need to follow to accomplish their goal. This may include teaching them to develop a clear and straightforward task analysis or step-by-step list for accomplishing the task. It may also include helping students think about general or broad considerations for preparing to work toward goal achievement. If task analytic instruction is needed, some students with ASD may need explicit instruction in how to identify or recognize steps. For students with extensive support needs, you may generate the steps of the plan and then provide modeling and guidance to help the student sequence the steps. It may be helpful for students to have a graphic organizer with numbered blank lines and premade steps they can affix in order. Some students may benefit from a backward chaining procedure where you model developing (or selecting) the first several steps of the task analysis and then give the student an opportunity to select the final step. This process can be repeated multiple times, with the student expected to complete more and more steps independently. Figure 1.7 shows an example of a goal-planning sheet for students with HFASD and students with ASD with more extensive cognitive support needs.

After students identify the steps for accomplishing their goal, teach them to consider any barriers that may impede their ability to access or use materials, complete steps, or perform the task with the greatest independence possible. Some students with ASD will benefit from a prelesson on the concept of *barriers*. Defining this term clearly and practicing with examples and nonexamples of barriers in different scenarios may help students develop a clear understanding of what barriers are and how they can be identified. For students with HFASD, a

Example for students with HFASD

Goal-Planning Worksheet

Part A: Materials

1. What materials do I need? _____

_____

_____

2. Are there choices I can make about my materials? _____

_____

_____

3. How will I get my materials? _____

_____

_____

Example for students with more extensive support needs

Goal-Planning Worksheet

Part A: Materials

1. What materials do I need?

| books | calculator | pencil | ruler |

2. How will I get my materials?

| my teacher | the classroom | other students | someone else |

Figure 1.6. Example of Part A of a goal-planning worksheet. The example for students with HFASD offers guiding questions for determining the types of materials needed, specifications of materials, and methods for locating materials. The example for students with more extensive support needs provides preselected, personalized response options. The wording and response options will vary based on the goal topics, and response options for possible materials may include examples/nonexamples.

Example for students with HFASD

Goal-Planning Worksheet

Part B: Steps for achieving my goal

My goal is to:

_____

_____

To meet my goal:

1. First, I will _____

_____

2. Next, I will: _____

_____

3. Last, I will: _____

_____

Example for students with more extensive support needs

Goal-Planning Worksheet

Part B: Steps for achieving my goal

My goal is to:

_____

_____

To meet my goal:

1st

1. First, I will _____

2nd

2. Next, I will _____

3rd

3. Last, I will _____

Response options for sequencing

(add specific steps plus picture supports as needed)

Figure 1.7. Example of Part B of a goal-planning worksheet. The example for students with HFASD utilizes prompts for sequencing steps to achieve a goal; these could include steps for preparing to do the target behavior, like making sure materials are ready. The example for students with more extensive support needs provides a response option bank with preselected steps. Students can cut and paste or copy steps and put them in order to complete their plan.

planning sheet with guiding questions can help them consider barriers. You can use think-aloud modeling to demonstrate how to consider whether barriers exist.

Finally, teach students to identify solutions for any potential barriers. This step includes being sure that students are aware of the supports that are available to them in the classroom, including how to access resources and how to elicit help from others. You can use think-aloud modeling to demonstrate how to consider the use of supports or resources to solve a problem or remove a barrier. For example, if the goal is to read two chapter books in 2 weeks, students may have identified that an important material would be the chapter books themselves. A potential barrier might be that the student has difficulty understanding what he is reading, even when he can decode the words easily. Based on prior experiences in the classroom, the student knows he can use the Kidspiration app on an iPad to record information about the story elements he is reading. The iPad makes it easy for him to quickly write down essential information about characters and setting; he can also receive audio prompts reminding him of the meaning of the different story elements by touching each word (e.g., plot, character, setting). Figure 1.8 provides an example of Part C of a goal-planning worksheet (identifying barriers and solutions to barriers).

Step 3: Developing a System for Measuring Progress Toward a Goal

Throughout our discussion of goal-setting interventions, we have examined the importance of teaching the goal-setting process through a gradual release of responsibility that begins with a high level of teacher control and input and ideally ends with student management. For Step 3, we recommend that teachers drive the development of a measurement system. The specifics of how to do this can be found in the next section on self-monitoring interventions. An important feature of goal-setting interventions is that we are teaching students to be more aware of the entire goal-setting process. Indeed, we want students to have an awareness of this entire process, including methods for measuring individual progress. Initially, strategies to consider for including students in this process can include structuring tools around their specific preferences and interests. For instance, if we teach students to monitor and record their progress toward a goal in 1-minute intervals, they can learn to record points or feedback using methods that match their interests. Maybe a student records 1 "Batman point" for every minute she is on task, because (a) she likes Batman and (b) she knows she is demonstrating focus and persistence with her math facts, just like Batman demonstrates focus and persistence when saving the people of Gotham City. Goal-setting interventions are all about planning and preparation, so for Step 3, developing a system for measuring progress toward goals, teachers have an opportunity to include students in the planning by incorporating specific interests or preferences.

Example for students with HFASD

Goal-Planning Worksheet

Part C: Overcoming barriers

When I think about my goal...

- What seems hard for me?
- What are things I have trouble doing by myself?
- What are things that make me want to give up?

Write possible <u>problems</u> in the table below.

When I think about getting help at school...

- Who can I ask for help?
- Where can I go to get things I need?
- What makes me want to keep trying?

Write possible <u>solutions</u> in the table below.

Problem	Solution

Example for students with more extensive support needs

Goal-Planning Worksheet

Part C: Overcoming barriers

When I think about my goal...

- What seems hard for me?
- What are things I have trouble doing by myself?
- What are things that make me want to give up?

Circle all possible <u>problems</u>:

| I don't like the sound the timer makes. | I don't like doing math. | I get sleepy when I do math. | I get confused with the numbers. |

Figure 1.8. Example of Part C of a goal-planning worksheet. The column on the left is an example of guided questions for considering possible barriers and solutions to barriers for students with HFASD. The column on the right is an example of a planning sheet with a response option bank for preselected barriers and solutions for students with ASD who have more extensive support needs. These barriers and solutions should be tailored to the specific needs and preferences of the student.

When I think about getting help at school...

• Who can I ask for help?
• Where can I go to get things I need?
• What makes me want to keep trying?

Circle all possible <u>solutions</u>:

			0 1 2 3 4 5 6 7 8 9 10
I can ask my teacher to help change the timer sound.	I can ask for a new reward for finishing my math.	I can ask my teacher for a resting break when I get tired.	I can go get a number line from the math materials.

Figure 1.8. (*continued*)

Step 4: Establishing Consequences

The final step in a goal-setting intervention is to establish clear consequences. The purpose of establishing consequences is to motivate students and increase the likelihood that the desired behavior or outcome will continue to occur in the future. A behavioral contract (also known as a contingency contract) is a good way to document the contingent relationship between the successful completion of a target behavior and access to a particular reinforcer (Cooper, Heron, & Heward, 2007). When used outside of goal-setting interventions, behavior contracts can be stand-alone documents that include a clear description of the target behavior (who will perform the goal, within what time frame, and to what criteria?) and a clear description of the reward (what is the reinforcer and how will it be accessed?). When used as part of a goal-setting intervention, this agreement about the relationship between the target behavior and access to a reinforcer can be added to the end of a goal-planning worksheet. It is important that both the teacher and the student agree upon the conditions of this contract. In order for the student to have meaningful input, teachers should conduct reinforcer inventories or preference assessments to gather data about the student's specific interests and preferences. This process is explained in greater detail in the final SMI section on self-reinforcement interventions.

Why Are Goal-Setting Interventions Important to Students With ASD?

Goal setting is the gateway to the self-management approach to instruction. By teaching students to set and plan their own goals, we are teaching them an important process that they may generalize beyond the classroom. It is this process that could have real utility for students beyond their school-age years, which is one reason why the content of the goal may not be as critical as the goal-setting process itself. Certainly, we hope to teach children to set goals that are meaningful and will result in increased academic, organizational, or prosocial behaviors. But we also have an opportunity to teach students a process for achieving something on their own. Ideally, through carefully designed instruction that transfers responsibility to the student incrementally over time, we can help students hone a skill that will impact them throughout adulthood. We want students with ASD to think about meaningful, attainable long-term goals, then identify related short-term goals that will help them along this path. We want students to identify the tools and materials they need to achieve their goal, as well as identify potential barriers that may deter their success. We want students to be able to thoughtfully develop a plan for mitigating or removing barriers and ultimately gaining the things they want out of life. Goal-setting interventions provide us, as educators, with an opportunity to lay this foundation for long-term student success.

What Are Self-Monitoring Interventions?

Self-monitoring interventions are the most widely utilized and most scientifically supported self-management interventions (SMIs; Lee et al., 2007). Self-monitoring interventions are also the most suited for use as a stand-alone intervention. While goal-setting approaches and self-reinforcement might have minor impact outside of a larger SMI package, self-monitoring has shown effectiveness when implemented as the primary mechanism for behavior change. As such, we describe self-monitoring with sufficient detail to be used as a stand-alone tool. Because of this autonomy, there are certain areas of overlap with the information presented previously in the goal-setting interventions section. Self-monitoring interventions involve the collecting and recording of data over time by the target individual. You can probably identify some ways in which you use self-monitoring in your daily life. Devices like Fitbits, calorie counters, sleep logs, and pedometers are all types of self-monitoring tools or systems. For example, you might have the short-term goal of exercising more frequently. To meet this goal, you download an app onto your smartphone that logs the frequency and duration of your exercise behavior. This app graphs this data over time, compares your performance from week to week and month to month, and dispenses rewards (e.g., congratulations, level achievements, and accomplishment sharing to social media). This process of recording, tracking, and reinforcing influences your decision to exercise more frequently.

Self-monitoring is effective for so many people because it is an active process that increases self-awareness and reminds the user of external criteria or specific goals they have set. Students with ASD benefit from self-monitoring in much the same way. The active process of recording and tracking features of their behavior often reduces problem behaviors and increases desired behaviors by cueing the student's attention to the presence of the targeted outcomes (Zirpoli, 2008). These behavioral improvements may be directly related to an increase in the student's self-awareness. As students become more self-aware, they begin to recognize the discrepancy between their behavior and other external norms (e.g., the behavior of others, specific instructor criteria). Other students with ASD likely benefit from the simple fact that they are receiving ongoing reminders from the monitoring system. These reminders serve as prompts to the students about features of their behavior and thereby reduce or improve behavior related to the targeted outcomes. Regardless of why these interventions work, the evidence is clear that self-monitoring interventions benefit many students with ASD.

Besides being effective, self-monitoring interventions can increase teacher capacity and student independence. These are tools that are designed to be managed by the target students, and they generally involve students collecting data on their own behavior. This process allows teachers to engage in other tasks in the classroom and provides opportunities for students to independently manage (i.e., evaluate and record) specific classroom behaviors. The resulting benefits of self-monitoring interventions are likely to resonate beyond the targeted students and the targeted behaviors and affect the classroom as whole. Clearly, self-monitoring represents a powerful evidence-based practice that makes sense for many students with ASD.

What Prerequisite Skills Do Students With ASD Need for Self-Monitoring Interventions?

It is our opinion that to benefit from a self-monitoring system, students with ASD should be able to (a) discriminate between occurrences and nonoccurrences of the target skill, (b) record these occurrences reliably and accurately over time, and (c) eventually manage the self-monitoring system (e.g., checklists, timers) independently. Students who are unable to demonstrate these skills can certainly be systematically taught to engage in these behaviors (the steps to teach these behaviors are outlined in the pages of this guide), and it is our belief that even students with ASD and cognitive impairments can benefit from self-monitoring systems. However, like all evidence-based practice implementation, selecting students who are likely to benefit from the prescribed treatment will lead to the most effective and efficient results. Similarly, in line with the consensus regarding implementation of effective practices, we believe that these monitoring systems should be developed for specific students after considering their cognitive, language, and functioning skills and deficits (Simpson & Myles, 2008).

Steps in Implementing Self-Monitoring Interventions

The process of developing self-monitoring interventions for students with ASD involves steps that should all be completed in a systematic and logical fashion. One of the benefits of self-monitoring systems is that they are flexible systems that can be developed in a variety of ways to meet the needs of specific students. In fact, research has shown a variety of self-monitoring approaches to be successful for students with autism. The downside to this flexibility can be adopting self-monitoring tools that are not developed systematically and thoughtfully for individual students and thus have little impact on student behavior. Therefore, we support the development of self-monitoring interventions by completing these steps in the order described. Clearly, each step in this process will not hold equal importance for every student, but carefully considering self-monitoring in this sequential and systematic fashion will lead to the best chance of success for the self-monitoring intervention you design. The steps covered in this guide are

1. selecting a target behavior or skill,
2. developing the self-monitoring system,
3. conducting student training,
4. implementing the self-monitoring system,
5. monitoring student progress,
6. enhancing and troubleshooting interventions,
7. fading the self-monitoring system, and
8. generalizing self-monitoring.

Step 1: Selecting a Target Behavior or Skill

The first step in developing a self-monitoring intervention is to choose a behavior that lends itself to ongoing self-monitoring. Fortunately, these interventions have proved to be effective in addressing a wide variety of targeted skills. Table 1.3 provides an indication of the evidence supporting self-monitoring interventions across targeted outcomes. As this table indicates, self-monitoring interventions have demonstrated effectiveness across a wide variety of behavioral outcomes, but this approach will almost certainly not work for all targeted outcomes. Behaviors that best lend themselves to self-monitoring include behaviors that occur frequently or need consistent monitoring, behaviors that have more distal consequences, and behaviors that are already in the student's repertoire (e.g., a performance deficit). For example, task-related behaviors (e.g., engagement, on task) often lend themselves to self-monitoring. This is because engagement requires constant or at least heightened attention—that is, the positive outcomes of

Table 1.3. Snapshot of the Self-Monitoring Evidence
Relative to Specific Outcomes

Increasing social and play skills	Increasing classroom routines	Decreasing problem behavior	Increasing task-related behavior	Increasing daily living proficiency
• Responding to peers • Nonverbal communication • Social initiations • Sharing • Appropriate play	• Following a schedule • Transitioning between activities • Following directions	• Disruptive behavior • Stereotypic behavior • Inappropriate vocalizations • Aggression	• Independent work skills • On task • Writing accuracy • Productivity • Academic accuracy	• Setting table • Making lunch • Getting dressed • Purchasing items from store

engagement are not realized until well after the fact (e.g., a grade on a test, weeks after studying for it)—and because many students often *can* engage in these behaviors, but frequently fail to demonstrate them consistently. Thankfully, many academic and prosocial behaviors meet these requirements, and the types of behaviors successfully addressed via self-monitoring are notably broad (Davis et al., 2016; Lee et al., 2007).

After you have selected a target behavior, you should work to carefully define the observable characteristics of the behavior and communicate this working definition (often referred to as an *operational definition*) to all stakeholders involved in the intervention (e.g., paraprofessionals, related service providers, the target student). This step is necessary because behaviors can be understood and defined in a variety of ways, and without an agreed-on definition, communication and data collection related to the target may be unreliable. While many guidelines exist for developing high-quality operational definitions, most agree that definitions should generally include the observable and measurable features of the behavior described with sufficient specificity to allow even unaffiliated observers to determine the occurrence or nonoccurrence of the behavior in question (Alberto & Troutman, 2012).

Once you have firmed up the operational definition of the target skill, it is essential that you develop a routine for collecting data on the occurrences of this behavior. The development of a data sheet and subsequent routines for collecting data will ultimately help you determine whether the intervention is working. You should begin this data collection process immediately by collecting baseline data points. These data points should be collected in the same environment that the self-monitoring intervention will be implemented, and you should collect at least 3–5 data points across subsequent days. Collecting baseline data not only helps you design a better monitoring system but also allows you to collect comparative data once you have designed and implemented the self-monitoring intervention.

Step 2: Developing the Self-Monitoring System

The self-monitoring system is the actual tool that students use to monitor and record their behavior over time. This multicomponent tool requires careful thought and planning. In order to successfully develop a self-monitoring system, you will need to (1) develop appropriate monitoring prompts, (2) select appropriate monitoring intervals, (3) determine timing and cueing mechanisms, and (4) design recording materials. We discuss each of these steps in the following pages.

Developing Appropriate Monitoring Prompts

As discussed, self-monitoring is an active, ongoing process in which students evaluate and record their own behavior. The initiating mechanism of this tool is the monitoring prompt. The monitoring prompt can take many forms, but in educational settings this prompt is often a *yes/no* question or a choice between descriptors or features of the student's behavior. The purpose of the monitoring prompt is to query a specific behavior or features of behavior directly connected to the targeted outcome. For example, if the targeted behavior was for the student to remain engaged during independent work activities, the monitoring question might be "Are you checked in?" or "Are you working?" Similarly, students could choose between two (or more) choices that best describe their engagement behavior (see Figure 1.9). Presenting the monitoring prompts this way requires the student to reflect on his or her own behavior and make an evaluation in the moment about whether the behavior meets the criterion referenced in the question or choice.

Because the monitoring question is the access point to the entire monitoring system, the prompt should be presented to students in a way that they can understand. If students are unable to process the monitoring question, then they are unlikely to benefit from the intervention. You can present monitoring prompts via complete sentences, phrases, single words, and/or pictures. Remember that the purpose of the monitoring prompt is to provide students with a concise query or choice directly connected to the targeted outcome. Figure 1.9 shows several sample monitoring prompts that are presented in a variety of ways to account for the variability in the processing abilities of students with ASD.

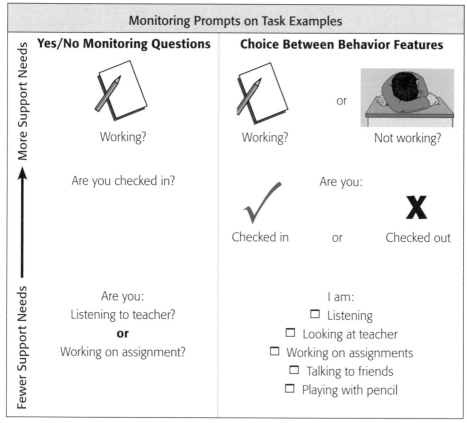

Figure 1.9. Monitoring prompt examples. This figure demonstrates different configurations and tiers of monitoring prompts. The column on the left demonstrates *Yes/No* monitoring questions, with supports for students with different abilities. The column on the right demonstrates monitoring prompts as a choice between features of behavior.

Clearly, you can use cueing systems other than a question as the monitoring prompt. Students can tally occurrences of behavior, rate their behavior on a predetermined (and prerehearsed) scale, complete a checklist describing features of their behavior, or simply choose between descriptors of their behavior. While it is unclear from the literature which of these mechanisms (e.g., questions, scales, checklists) will work best for which students, it is our opinion that you should tailor the monitoring prompt specifically to the target student. Work directly with students to identify their preferences and determine what they are able to process without teacher support. After all, if the true benefits of self-monitoring interventions are to be realized, then students must be able to use these systems independently. If in doubt, it is best to start with a simple monitoring question. This approach will be straightforward for many students, and adjustments can be made to incorporate other types of monitoring prompts as students become more familiar with the self-monitoring system.

Selecting Appropriate Monitoring Intervals

Once you have established the monitoring prompt, it is time to determine how frequently the student will be cued to respond to the monitoring prompt. This is an important consideration: If you cue the student too frequently, he or she is likely to be annoyed by the constant reminders and ultimately distracted by the system. However, if you do not sufficiently cue the student, the intervention will have little impact. As we consider how frequently to cue the student, it is an appropriate time to think about two types of self-monitoring. These two types are not well defined in the literature, but for lack of better phrasing let us refer to these types as *noncued self-monitoring* and *ongoing self-monitoring*. Noncued self-monitoring encompasses a variety of self-monitoring approaches, including self-monitoring that involves the student recording frequency of behaviors (e.g., counting the number of talk-outs) and self-monitoring that cues the student to respond to the monitoring prompt at the end of an event, class period, social interaction, or school day. This type of self-monitoring might be appropriate for certain students and certain behaviors.

For example, it might be appropriate for behaviors that naturally occur infrequently (e.g., turning in homework, having necessary materials), naturally occur at the end of an event (e.g., appropriate transitioning, putting away materials), or are discrete behaviors best measured by counting (e.g., talking out). This type of self-monitoring might also be more appropriate for students with cognitive skills in the normal range, who can reflect on their behavior over longer periods of time. This type of self-monitoring is used a great deal in classrooms, and certain "check-in" or exit ticket procedures certainly model this type of student reflection on their behavior. However, this is not the type of self-monitoring that should be utilized initially for most behaviors, especially those that occur infrequently, generally lack specific routines, and often have little teacher or adult oversight. Rather, practitioners should look to this type of self-monitoring as the ultimate goal of ongoing self-monitoring. That is, as students learn about self-monitoring and demonstrate accuracy and independence when using self-monitoring systems, we can fade the ongoing nature of self-monitoring and have students "check-in" periodically with self-monitoring data. Figure 1.10 shows two types of student recording materials for noncued self-monitoring.

We suggest that initially most behaviors be addressed using ongoing self-monitoring, even if the initial intervals are long (e.g., 10 minutes or more). Ongo-

	Today in math class, did I . . . ?		✓
• Follow directions		yes ☐	no ☐
• Complete activities		yes ☐	no ☐
• Keep my body quiet		yes ☐	no ☐
• Stay safe with my body and words		yes ☐	no ☐

Class	During class I was . . .			
Communication Arts	Working?	Yes	No	
	Awake?	Yes	No	
	Do I have homework?	Yes	No	N/A
	Did I write it in my planner?	Yes	No	N/A
	Did I turn in _____?	Yes	No	N/A
American History	Working?	Yes	No	
	Awake?	Yes	No	
	Do I have homework?	Yes	No	N/A
	Did I write it in my planner?	Yes	No	N/A
	Did I turn in _____?	Yes	No	N/A

Figure 1.10. Two examples of noncued self-monitoring. In each example, students respond to *Yes/No* questions about their behavior at the end of a specific class.

ing self-monitoring involves establishing consistent intervals of time and presenting the monitoring prompt to the student at the end of each time interval. The frequency of these intervals should be a function of the current rate of the behavior and the context in which you are implementing the intervention. Behaviors that occur at a high rate (e.g., stereotypic behaviors) or are continuous in nature (e.g., engagement) should be cued more frequently (e.g., every 1–3 minutes). In contrast, behaviors that occur less frequently lend themselves to more periodic cueing (e.g., every 3–15 minutes, depending on the behavior). Relative to the context in which the intervention will be implemented, keep in mind that some environments lend themselves to frequent or ongoing cueing (e.g., independent work) and others may require more prudent use of cueing intervals (e.g., recess). Figure 1.11 presents two examples of ongoing self-monitoring materials.

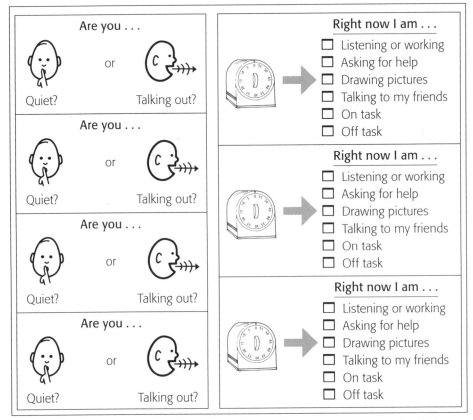

Figure 1.11. Two examples of ongoing self-monitoring. At the end of each interval, the student responds to the monitoring prompt.

Determining Timing and Cueing Mechanisms

Now that you have determined the exact monitoring prompt and decided on a cueing interval, you need to choose some technology or other means to manage the intervals and remind the student to respond to the monitoring prompt. The purpose of this tool is to bring the student's awareness to the monitoring prompt, specifically, per the intervals you have set. For example, if you identified engagement as the target behavior and have decided that 3-minute intervals are appropriate, then you need something to manage those intervals and remind the student to consider the monitoring prompt. There are many timing and cueing mechanisms available, such as stand-alone timers, smart phone apps, or even browser-based software. An Internet search provides a variety of cost-effective options. These are some features to look for:

- is easy to use
- includes volume control to reduce distraction

- has a vibrate-only feature
- allows for multiple timed intervals
- allows for customized intervals (e.g., as with high-intensity interval training [HIIT] fitness apps)

In truth, there are many tools that will reliably cue students to attend to the monitoring prompt, including many we have not discussed. The key is to select a tool that the student can be successfully trained to use independently and that is appropriate for the space. As we have already stated numerous times, if the student cannot manage the monitoring system independently, then you will not be realizing the full value of this intervention.

Designing Recording Materials

Remember that self-monitoring involves students evaluating and recording their own behavior over time. The process of recording should always be developed with the student in mind. Recording materials generally include the monitoring prompt and a space or means for the students to record their behavior. Figure 1.12 shows several student recording forms currently being utilized by classroom teachers. The key to success is to develop these recording forms in intuitive ways that align with learners' needs and characteristics and in a manner that supports student independence.

Another point to make about the recording materials is that students should track their behavior over time. This can include making graphs and reviewing progress on an ongoing basis. This process helps students visualize improvements in their behavior. This recording procedure can also be intrinsically motivating for many students. Similarly, these gains can be further incentivized by the introduction of extrinsic reinforcement at specific behavioral thresholds (see Figure 1.13). Graphs can be developed in Excel or other graphing software. One iOS application that is simple and easy for many students to navigate is Easy Chart HD. Regardless of which graphing program you use, recognize that this is an underutilized and essential feature of self-monitoring systems.

Step 3: Conducting Student Training

Once you have selected a target behavior and designed the monitoring system, you will need to spend some time training students to use and manage the system accurately and independently. This step is often overlooked by practitioners seeking to implement self-monitoring systems. Keep in mind that these systems will not work as intended without systematic student training. When training students to use self-monitoring, you should train them to (a) accurately

1. When the timer goes off have you been ...

	Working?		Having on-topic comments or questions?		Staying in your own space?	
⏱	Yes	No	Yes	No	Yes	No
⏱	Yes	No	Yes	No	Yes	No
⏱	Yes	No	Yes	No	Yes	No
⏱	Yes	No	Yes	No	Yes	No
⏱	Yes	No	Yes	No	Yes	No
⏱	Yes	No	Yes	No	Yes	No
⏱	Yes	No	Yes	No	Yes	No
⏱	Yes	No	Yes	No	Yes	No
Total Yes Circles:						

_____ Yes gets 15 minutes of _____ time.

2.

🤝 😐	**YES**	**NO**	
Cool hands and voice?			

_____ 🐟 = _____

3.

Date: _____

Are you on task?

😊	**YES**
😢	**NO**

Figure 1.12. Examples of student recording materials currently being used by classroom teachers. In Example 1, a student with high-functioning autism is monitoring several behaviors each interval; in Example 2, a student with autism and cognitive impairments is monitoring occurrences of appropriate behavior by moving a Velcro fish (a specific interest for this student); and Example 3 demonstrates a simple monitoring prompt for an adolescent with ASD using emoji icons.

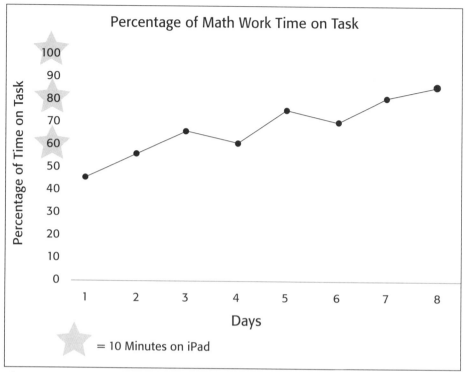

Figure 1.13. An example of how self-monitoring data could be collected over time and displayed with specific reinforcement thresholds.

discriminate between occurrences and nonoccurrences of their behavior (or to recognize relevant features of their behavior) and (b) manage and use the system without prompts (e.g., respond to the monitoring prompt, manage the cueing device, etc.). These are two distinct training outcomes; however, we recommend training these two concepts together, using the methods of incidental teaching and the principles of systematic instruction. Before you begin the training sessions, it is best to develop criteria for both of these training outcomes. It is important to establish these criteria, as this will let you know when the student has mastered these prerequisites to self-monitoring.

Developing Training Criteria

When developing training criteria, you are essentially setting a goal for the student training session(s). If a student cannot be taught to discriminate accurately and independently, there are perhaps better supports for this student than self-monitoring interventions. The first criterion to set is related to the level of accuracy students demonstrate when recording features of their behavior. Unfortunately, the research literature is not entirely clear on the relevant contribution of accuracy of self-recording. That is, students (and individuals in general) can benefit from self-monitoring (i.e., their behavior can change) even if they are not accurately reporting levels of their behavior. For example, if you are trying to lose weight and are using a calorie counter and an exercise tracker as a means of self-monitoring, you can absolutely report results that are not accurate (in fact, the research suggests most people are not 100% accurate in their self-reporting), and you can still benefit from self-monitoring because you are being cued to attend to the larger goal of losing weight. In short, this active reflection on your actions (eating and exercise) can certainly change your behavior even if you are fudging the numbers a little. What is important is that you have a general sense of what these activities (eating and exercise) entail and your recording is reasonably accurate and in touch with what is happening in reality.

For students with ASD, it is our opinion that they should be taught to record as accurately as possible, and we recommend setting an accuracy-of-self-recording criterion of 80% during the training sessions. We believe that this relatively high level of accuracy will allow students the best chance of deriving value from the self-monitoring intervention. Of course, this could be adjusted for specific students, and we have personally documented students benefiting from self-monitoring with lower levels of accuracy (see Crutchfield et al., 2015). We discuss how to measure accuracy in the training scenarios presented below.

After you have established the accuracy threshold for the student, you will need to establish an acceptable level of independence. *Independence* refers to how self-sufficiently the student uses the specific components of the self-monitoring tool (i.e., the recording and the cueing materials). The goal should be for the student to use the tool with high levels of independence during the training session. Similarly, you should continue to probe the level of independence from time to time during the implementation of the self-monitoring intervention to ensure that the student is continuing to use the system independently (more on this in the implementation section). We recommend that the independence threshold be set at 90% during the training sessions. We discuss how to measure independence in the training scenarios presented below.

Training Scenarios

Once you have arrived at accuracy and independence thresholds, you should begin to instruct students on the discrimination between occurrences and nonoccurrences of the target behavior and the subsequent use of the monitoring tool. How this instruction is accomplished will, of course, depend on the learning characteristics of the specific student. However, in order to provide some training guidelines, we have created two training scenarios. Scenario #1 represents a proposed training session for a student with ASD who has minimal support needs, can use and process complex verbal language, and has an IQ in the normal range (i.e., similar to Asperger syndrome or high-functioning autism). Scenario #2 presents a proposed training session for a student with more significant support needs, who does not use spontaneous verbal language and has an intellectual disability. From these two bookends, you can calibrate the training sessions to meet the needs of specific students.

Training Scenario #1. Conduct the training session in the same setting and during the same activity in which you hope to implement the self-monitoring intervention. Begin the training by showing all the materials to the student, and provide a brief rationale for the intervention. Use the principles of model–lead–test to teach the student to monitor his own behavior accurately and independently. Begin the model phase by providing the student with a complete model of the monitoring system. When the cueing mechanism indicates the end of the interval, respond to the monitoring prompt, while discussing with the student what you are doing. Model at least three intervals, and include examples and nonexamples of the target response. This will ensure that you and the student can discuss behaviors that are included within the operational definition.

Once you have modeled three intervals, continue to the lead phase of instruction. In this phase, allow the student to use the monitoring system. Give the student an associated task, and instruct him to work on the task and answer the monitoring prompt at the end of each interval. Provide the student with prompts and suggestions as you go. For example, if he answers the monitoring question incorrectly, provide some feedback, instructing him on why his response was incorrect. Similarly, if he does not respond to the monitoring prompt at the end of a cueing interval, prompt him to answer the question or record the relevant feature of his behavior. Practice these procedures with the student for at least five intervals.

In the test phase, you want the student to use the system by himself, and thus you should take data on his accuracy and independence levels. During the test phase, keep a copy of the student's monitoring materials and complete the materials yourself at the end of each cueing interval, then compare your responses to the student's responses. Inaccurate responses (e.g., responses on which you and the student disagree) should count against the student's accuracy level, and instances of nonresponse from the student should count against the independence level of the student. Once the student is able to respond to approximately 80% of the intervals with accurate responses and approximately 80% of the intervals independently (or at whatever thresholds you have set), then you can begin implementing the self-monitoring intervention. These phases of training (model–lead–test) can take place across multiple days or during one training session. Students will generally pick up the use of these systems quickly when they are presented in this manner.

Training Scenario #2. For a student with more extensive support needs, you may need to embed visual supports and systematic instruction within the model–lead–test format. The overall instructional approach is similar to that in Scenario #1, but additional supports and response-prompt procedures will help promote maintenance and generalization of self-monitoring skills. For a student with ASD who also has communication and cognitive support needs, it is important to ensure that the training procedures and materials include receptive response modes and systematic supports. For a detailed description of how to teach these procedures to a student with ASD and/or an intellectual disability (ID), see Nathan's case study example at the end of Part One.

Step 4: Implementing the Self-Monitoring Intervention

Now that you have identified the behavior(s) to target, developed the associated monitoring system, and trained the student to use the monitoring system accurately and independently, it is time to implement the monitoring intervention. This is a simple step in which the student begins to monitor the target behavior in the relevant context. One important implementation guideline is to use specific error correction procedures. No matter how thoroughly you have trained the student, she is likely to need additional prompts regarding the accuracy of her self-record and her levels of independence, especially in the beginning. We recommend carefully observing the student the first two or three times she uses the monitoring system and employing the following error correction procedures when necessary.

The general rule of the error correction procedure is that you should not allow the student to respond to the monitoring prompt inaccurately or not respond at all for more than one interval. For example, if the student is monitoring her on-task behavior, the monitoring prompt is "Are you working?," and the monitoring interval is set to 3 minutes, you should position yourself close to the student so that you can observe her response to the monitoring prompt. If she does not respond to the prompt or responds inaccurately (e.g., indicates she is working when in fact she is not), on the first interval you would not intervene at all. However, if the same error or nonresponse is repeated on the next interval, you would immediately intervene and correct the error. (Specific error correction scripts are modeled in the case study at the end of Part One.) This error correction ensures that the student does not develop faulty self-monitoring habits. If you must use the error correction routinely, then we recommend that you introduce additional training or booster sessions to retrain the student on accurate self-recording or independent use of the monitoring system.

Step 5: Monitoring Student Progress

Once the intervention has been implemented and the student is using the intervention without the need for ongoing error correction, you should begin to assess the impact of the intervention tool on the target behavior. You should do this by collecting observational data in the same way you compiled baseline data. You can compare these data visually in graphed form and thus evaluate the overall effect of the self-monitoring intervention. One thing to keep in mind is that self-monitoring interventions can demonstrate a "dosage effect." This means that you might not see an immediate improvement in behavior and the intervention might need to be used over time for the effects to be noticed. We recommend that you collect at least 5 data points before deciding on next steps. After collecting these data points, you should have a good indication of whether the self-monitoring system is successfully addressing the target behavior. If the system is working as intended, then you should skip to Step 7 and begin working to fade the intervention over time. If the intervention is not working, or you think it could be working better, then you should review the enhancing and troubleshooting options presented in Step 6.

Step 6: Enhancing and Troubleshooting Self-Monitoring Interventions

Many interventions that we implement for students with ASD may not be immediately successful. This could be due to a variety of factors, including individual student characteristics, implementation errors, or contextual variables. When interventions do not work as intended (especially those that science has indicated often do work for students with ASD), we should not abandon them immediately, but rather we should try to enhance these approaches or troubleshoot elements of the intervention to see if it can achieve the desired effects for the students in our care. When self-monitoring interventions are not working as intended, two actions that research suggests might be helpful are (a) packaging the self-monitoring system with positive reinforcement and (b) using video-based tools to teach additional discrimination or monitoring skills. These suggestions are discussed below.

Packaging Positive Reinforcement and Self-Management

Positive reinforcement is one of the most powerful consequence strategies at our disposal and can be packaged with many evidence-based practices to enhance their effectiveness. When packaging positive reinforcement, we can positively reinforce the actual behavior of self-monitoring (e.g., responding to the monitoring prompt) or we can positively reinforce demonstration of the target behavior. Relative to the first option, many students do not derive benefit from the self-monitoring system because they are not actually engaging in self-monitoring, due to a lack of response to the monitoring prompt. The error correction procedures described in Step 4 should address this; however, if students still demonstrate difficulty independently responding to the monitoring prompt, you might consider providing positive reinforcement when students engage in independent monitoring. This should be structured so that students receive positive reinforcement during the monitoring intervals in the form of secondary reinforcers (e.g., tokens), which they can exchange for primary reinforcers at the end of the target task.

Similarly, if students are engaging in the self-monitoring routines but their behavior is not moving in the desired direction, you can provide positive reinforcement related to the target behavior. To accomplish this, simply establish specific reinforcement criteria and include these as part of the student recording materials (see Figure 1.14). A word of caution: Attaching reinforcement to the targeted response may change the student's accuracy of self-recording. For example, if you establish the criterion that a student must be on task for six out of the seven monitoring intervals, the student may begin to report that he is on task, even when he is not, to gain access to the reinforcer. To manage this, we would encourage you to collect accuracy of self-recording data whenever you introduce positive reinforcement connected to the target behavior. Once the student has demonstrated that he can record accurately, even when it might influence his access to reinforcement, you can fade your oversight of his self-recording. You should also consider systematically increasing the criterion to receive reinforcement until you are able to fade reinforcement altogether and the student can maintain appropriate levels of the target behavior with the use of the self-monitoring system alone.

Using Video-Based Tools to Enhance Self-Monitoring

Another set of tools that researchers have successfully packaged with self-monitoring systems is video based, including video modeling and video feedback (see Crutchfield et al., 2015). One reason that video-based tools are so nicely packaged with self-monitoring systems is that video-based tools provide instruction and feedback to the student that are not directly delivered by a teacher or other classroom adult. These efficient and effective tools can be used to assist students in the self-monitoring routine and can also assist students in evaluating their own behavior. One way to use video tools is to create a self-video model that shows the student accurately and independently using the self-monitoring system. The

1-Hour Studying Self-Monitoring

Did you study for your test MOST of the time in this interval?	Did you study for your test MOST of the time in this interval?
☐ Yes ☐ No — First 15 minutes	☐ Yes ☐ No — Second 15 minutes
Did you study for your test MOST of the time in this interval?	Did you study for your test MOST of the time in this interval?
☐ Yes ☐ No — Third 15 minutes	☐ Yes ☐ No — Last 15 minutes

3 yes answers = 15 minutes of video games

Figure 1.14. Reinforcement criteria clearly displayed on the self-recording materials.

best way to do this is to record several sessions of the student using the self-monitoring intervention, then edit out all the instances of error correction and any missed intervals (you could also edit out any occurrences or nonoccurrences of the target behavior). This model can then be viewed by the student, and he or she will see not only independent use of the monitoring system but also appropriate levels of the target behavior.

If the student is demonstrating difficulty with self-evaluation, usually manifested by inconsistent or inaccurate self-recording, you can use the video feedback tool to help provide additional instruction. Video feedback is an instructional technique wherein students watch videos of themselves and evaluate their behavior based on specific criteria (Deitchman, Reeve, Reeve, & Progar, 2010). When using video feedback with a self-monitoring system, students should watch brief examples and nonexamples of the target behavior and then respond to the monitoring prompt. For example, if you were trying to reduce the frequency of talking out behavior during whole group instruction, you could show the student a clip of her working quietly and then have her respond to the monitoring prompt "Were you working quietly?" Similarly, you could show an instance of talking out behavior and then ask her to again respond to the monitoring prompt, providing additional instruction or cueing as you go. Importantly, we do *not* recommend

that you use video feedback when trying to reduce aggression or self-injurious behaviors, as there are certainly ethical concerns with showing students instances
of themselves engaging in harmful behaviors. Video feedback is particularly useful when implementing self-monitoring with students who have limited verbal
language capabilities or who might have an ASD and a cognitive impairment.
This technique does not require the student to process verbal language; none-
theless, it can successfully teach students to identify occurrences and nonoccurrences of specific behavior.

Step 7: Fading the Self-Monitoring System

Any formal intervention system, even those that have the potential to increase
the self-management skills of students with ASD, should be systematically faded
whenever possible. Self-monitoring systems, when developed in the way that we
have described, can be very easy to fade. Once the target behavior has reached an
appropriate level, simply increase the interval timing to cue the student to self-
monitor on a less frequent basis. This can be accomplished regardless of the interval length. We recommend that you begin by increasing the cueing interval by
50% while continuing to monitor the effects on the target behavior. For example,
if the student was responding to the monitoring prompt at 3-minute intervals,
simply increase the cueing interval by 50% of the initial interval, or 1.5 minutes.
The new cueing interval would then be every 4.5 minutes. This process could be
continued until the student was monitoring at the end of the class period or the
end of the school day. Of course, if the student's behavior returned to unaccept-
able levels, then you could decrease the monitoring interval to the last successful
cueing interval.

Step 8: Generalizing the Self-Monitoring System

Generalizing the self-monitoring system is an important, simple step that is often
overlooked with SMI. As students increase the skill and consistency of their monitoring, you should look to implement self-monitoring systems across behaviors
and environments. This can be a straightforward process of extending current
monitoring systems that students already know how to use to new environments
or new behaviors. Similarly, as students increase their skill in self-monitoring,
you can extend the monitoring systems to more complex behaviors. Start by identifying an additional environment where the target behavior is still a relevant
concern. Make the monitoring materials available to the student in the new environment, and then conduct periodic data collection to ensure the monitoring

skills are transferring. Then look to extend the monitoring system to other behaviors that lend themselves to self-monitoring.

The guidelines detailed here are by no means the only way to implement self-monitoring interventions. Researchers have demonstrated that self-monitoring tools are flexible, dynamic systems that can be calibrated for individual students and environments. Therefore, it is important to keep in mind that many students will pick up self-monitoring intuitively, and the steps we have outlined may not be necessary for all students. However, it is our hope that these guidelines will help you consider all elements of self-monitoring, and thereby develop more effective and efficient self-monitoring tools.

What Are Self-Reinforcement Interventions?

In contrast to self-monitoring interventions, self-reinforcement interventions are an SMI with less empirical backing, particularly for students with ASD. These interventions are also likely to be included as part of an SMI package as opposed to serving as stand-alone interventions. For example, Stahmer and Schreibman (1992) taught elementary-age students with ASD and ID to demonstrate appropriate play behaviors through a packaged intervention that included self-monitoring and self-reinforcement components. Self-reinforcement includes identifying effective reinforcers or rewards, determining whether and when reinforcers should be delivered, and independently accessing reinforcers. The ability to deliver one's own extrinsic rewards can be very helpful for promoting personal achievement. For example, when engaging in difficult or aversive tasks, we can often motivate ourselves and increase our own persistence when we have control over our own rewards. The anticipated reward of going on vacation is typically a strong motivator to go to work every day and earn money. If we have selected a highly preferred vacation destination (which ideally is the case), we are more likely to engage in behaviors that will result in earning our paychecks (and perhaps even overtime compensation). By rewarding ourselves with a beachside resort vacation, we have reinforced the likelihood that we will continue to work diligently at our jobs in the future.

There is some evidence that suggests that students with ASD can learn to successfully use self-reinforcement interventions (Lee et al., 2007). Also worth noting, most of the student participants with ASD included in the body of extant research had mild to moderate ID (e.g., Reinecke, Newman, & Meinberg, 1999; Stahmer & Schreibman, 1992). Despite the limited evidence, it is reasonable to consider the use of self-reinforcement strategies for students with ASD. Potential self-regulatory benefits of self-reinforcement practices include greater student engagement, increased self-awareness, and opportunities to practice delayed gratification. As with most people, students with ASD may be more invested in an SMI if they know they will be able to deliver their own reinforcement. Through deliberate instruction in the steps of self-reinforcement, students with ASD will also have an opportunity to increase self-awareness through reinforcement inventories. Finally, if students with ASD receive instruction in the features and purpose of intermittent schedules of reinforcement, they may increase their capacity and willingness to delay gratification and exercise greater self-control and flexibility.

What Prerequisite Skills Do Students With ASD Need for Self-Reinforcement Interventions?

It is our opinion that to benefit from a self-reinforcement system, students with ASD should be able to (a) discriminate between preferred items and nonpreferred items, (b) evaluate their own behavior and make a determination as to when behavioral thresholds have been met, and (c) wait to exchange secondary reinforcers (i.e., tokens) for other primary or secondary reinforcers. Students who are unable to demonstrate these skills can certainly be systematically taught to engage in these behaviors (the steps to teach these behaviors are outlined in the pages of this guide), and it is our belief that students with ASD, including those with ASD and cognitive impairment(s), can benefit from self-reinforcement interventions. However, like all evidence-based-practice implementation, selecting students who are likely to benefit from the prescribed treatment will lead to the most effective and efficient results.

Steps in Implementing Self-Reinforcement Interventions

The basic steps in self-reinforcement interventions are

1. conducting a reinforcement inventory,
2. supporting self-evaluation, and
3. establishing a schedule for reinforcement and fading.

As in the previous sections, we offer these steps as suggested practices for teaching students with ASD with or without extensive support needs to actively participate in self-reinforcement procedures. As in previous sections, we recommend general procedures of explicit instruction for all students (including a gradual release of responsibility across time). For students with more extensive support needs, look for ways to embed more rigorous systematic instructional procedures (e.g., constant time delay, shaping) and example/nonexample training as needed. Let us now consider specific instructional considerations for each step of self-reinforcement interventions.

Step 1: Conducting a Reinforcement Inventory

Any reinforcement system (teacher directed or student directed) should begin with an analysis of student preferences. If students do not value the reward they receive following an appropriate demonstration of a target behavior, the reward is not actually *rewarding*. To ensure that we are providing access to true reinforcers, we must help students consider their likes and dislikes. This step of self-reinforcement procedures also allows teachers the opportunity to help students gain awareness of the nature of their own behaviors. Students may benefit from understanding concepts like *satiation* (that one can become tired of a reinforcer through overexposure). For students with more extensive support needs, this level of understanding might include teaching them to create their own menu of reinforcers by picking two or three highly preferred items. By not only providing students with a choice of reinforcers but also encouraging them to select and consider their own array of choices, we may help students avoid satiation.

When we develop or select response options for reinforcement inventories, it is helpful to consider some basic guidelines about reinforcers. First, we should do our best to offer reinforcers that are age appropriate, even if students express strong interest in particular objects or behaviors. For example, if a high school student loves trains, it is probably not appropriate to offer *Thomas the Train* stickers as generalized conditioned reinforcers (i.e., tokens or points that can be traded for access to primary or secondary reinforcers) or offer access to watching clips from *Thomas the Train* (a secondary reinforcer). These options would be more appropriate for elementary-age students. Instead, offer T points (the letter T can serve as an age-appropriate generalized conditioned reinforcer, and this may be motivating because it is still associated with trains), or offer access to real-life clips of locomotives on YouTube. While primary and secondary reinforcers may account for many of the types of reinforcers you include on a reinforcement inventory, be sure to include social reinforcers as well. Social reinforcers include expressions (e.g., high fives, thumbs-up, pats on the back), proximity (e.g., access to preferred peers or adults), and privileges or activities (e.g., extended lunchtime, a homework pass, extra computer time, free choice).

After developing a reinforcement inventory based on (a) your knowledge of the student and (b) various categories of reinforcers, ensure that the student understands the concepts necessary for indicating a preference. This includes understanding the concepts of "I like" and "I don't like," as well as "I like this the *most*." Students with HFASD may be able to circle all preferred items from a list and then rank-order them, given explicit instructions and modeling of these two steps. Students with more extensive support needs may benefit from example/ nonexample training in prerequisite concepts ("I like," "I don't like," "I like this the *most*"). Students with HFASD may be able to indicate preferences for reinforcers given a straightforward worksheet with choices. Other students may benefit from a structured teacher-led session of selecting from an array of picture/word cards. In this format, present students with option cards and ask them to identify the ones they like and the ones they do not like. After eliminating unwanted cards, present two preferred reinforcement cards at a time and ask students to identify the card they like the most. Continue this activity until you have identified a bank of reinforcers and have the ones that are most preferred. As mentioned earlier in this section, we can promote maintenance and generalization of concepts such as "I like" and "I don't like" by involving students in the selection of reinforcers for each SMI. When students help construct behavior contracts, consider asking them to select two or three choices for their reinforcement by selecting from re- inforcers "I like." Students with less extensive support needs may simply be told to "choose two to three options for your reward" when building their behavior contracts. By teaching students to select from things they have identified as high- preference reinforcers and constructing their own menu of choices, we can pro- mote increased independence in self-reinforcement interventions.

Step 2: Supporting Self-Evaluation

Considerations for teaching students to self-evaluate were described in the pre- vious section on self-monitoring interventions. To briefly reiterate the critical features of this component of SMIs, remember to train students to accurately determine whether they have met predetermined behavioral thresholds. The ac- curacy of their evaluation is important, both for the success of the SMI and for promoting generalization of self-reinforcement behaviors in future contexts. Students who have not been taught to make accurate evaluations may gain easy access to a preferred reinforcer in a school context, but this behavior is not likely to generalize to nonschool and postschool contexts. For instance, if a student performs a task at school and decides to access a reinforcer despite performing the task poorly, the student may learn that quality does not matter. This same student is likely to be disappointed when a future employer fires him or docks his salary when he does not meet quality standards for job tasks. When designing and implementing self-reinforcement interventions, be sure to follow the recom- mendations for teaching evaluation (from the section on self-monitoring interventions) and provide prompts as needed to remind students to continue to accurately evaluate their progress.

Step 3: Establishing a Schedule for Reinforcement and Fading

While we can teach students to systematically deliver and fade their own reinforcement, an overarching goal of this step of the process is to help students understand the power of rewards. The purpose of self-reinforcement is not to allow students free access to reinforcers at any time. Students should recognize (through teacher explanation and think-aloud modeling) that one reason we have schedules of delivery is to ensure that growth is happening along the way. Teachers should explain the concept of *contingency* (delivery of X reward is *contingent* on the performance or absence of X behavior). The Premack Principle (*first* you do ___, *then* you get ___) is a basic way of demonstrating the importance of successfully completing a task in order to gain a desired consequence. Students may be easily convinced to deliver reinforcement to themselves on a continuous schedule of reinforcement (for *every* instance of the target behavior, I get a reward), but part of our job at this step is to ensure we provide students with opportunities to practice staggered and intermittent schedules of reinforcement that will better ensure maintenance of the target behavior over time.

We want students to recognize the planning required to develop a delivery system that is both manageable and effective. It is not necessary to teach students with ASD to understand the nuances of different schedules of reinforcement. Instead, using the gradual release of responsibility approach, teachers can (and should) begin self-reinforcement instruction by establishing schedules of reinforcement that allow for fading over time. Eventually, if students are successful at delivering their own reinforcement according to the conditions of a teacher-directed schedule of reinforcement, it would make sense to begin teaching them to make instructional decisions about schedules of reinforcement (and how to systematically fade them over time). Instructional procedures that may help in teaching students with ASD to develop their own schedules of reinforcement include the *systematic fading of explicit modeling* of the delivery of reinforcement, *think-aloud modeling* of why we would choose specific schedules of delivery, *visual supports of task analytic procedures* for selecting and using reinforcement schedules, and *prompts* for fading delivery of reinforcement over time.

In order for teachers to help students understand the overarching concepts of schedules and systematic fading, teachers themselves must have a firm understanding of effective reinforcement procedures. While a continuous schedule of reinforcement (reinforcing every target behavior) is a powerful way to teach new behaviors, these are not the intended targets of self-management interventions.

Instead, students who are learning to manage their own behaviors will benefit most from intermittent schedules of reinforcement, wherein some (but not all) correct or appropriate target behaviors are reinforced. Intermittent reinforcement can be categorized as ratio or interval. For ratio schedules of reinforcement, the number of times reinforcement is delivered is determined by the number of times a target behavior occurs. For interval schedules of reinforcement, behaviors are rewarded when there is an occurrence of at least one correct response in conjunction with the passing of a specified amount of time. Both ratio and interval schedules of reinforcement are intended to increase the frequency of a target behavior. Benefits of intermittent schedules of reinforcement include (a) satiation is avoided (students are less likely to become tired of the reinforcer), (b) behaviors are more resistant to extinction, (c) students may learn to delay gratification, and (d) behaviors tend to maintain over longer periods of time. Specific definitions and examples of intermittent schedules of reinforcement are shown in Table 1.4.

Why Are Self-Reinforcement Interventions Important to Students With ASD?

Some research suggests student-delivered reinforcement is just as effective as teacher-delivered reinforcement (Newman, Buffington, & Hemmes, 1996). We know that students with ASD *can* learn to deliver their own reinforcement, but if this approach is equally as effective when delivered by adults, what is the value of investing time in these student-directed training procedures? While this form of SMI has been the subject of relatively little empirical research, the possible value of teaching students with ASD to deliver their own reinforcement echoes what we have suggested throughout this manual: Teaching students with ASD to manage their own behaviors may lead to increased overall quality of life and independence. If we can teach students to reinforce their own behaviors across contexts, they will be that much better prepared to reinforce their own behaviors in adulthood. If we can teach them to consider their own preferences, make accurate evaluative decisions about their progress, and reinforce their own behaviors thoughtfully and systematically over time, they will have gained a crucial tool for promoting personal growth, independence, and success across their life span.

Self-Management Case Study

Introduction

The three primary components of SMIs have been presented in three distinct sections on goal setting, self-monitoring, and self-reinforcement. Within each

Table 1.4. Definitions and Examples of Intermittent Schedules of Reinforcement

Schedule type	Definition	School example	Real-life example
Fixed ratio (e.g., FR 3)	• Requires completion of a set number of responses • Watch out for postreinforcement pause • Often produces high rate of response (person controls payoff!) • Size of ratio matters: higher ratio usually equals higher rate of response	Student receives a happy face sticker after learning 5 new sight words Student receives a break for every 10 math problems completed	Paid for each job you complete (earning commission for each sale; e.g., selling houses, selling cars)
Variable ratio (e.g., VR 10)	• Requires completion of a variable number of responses • First, identify the average number of responses • Then, select a maximum ratio (say, 15 responses) • Next, use a table of random numbers to identify specific variable ratios (that range from 1 to the maximum you selected) • The average of the random numbers is the number for your schedule • Tends to produce a quick rate of responses • Tends to produce a consistent, steady rates of responses	Tic-tac-toe VR: Pick a maximum number for the group (a higher number will mean a longer time to pay off). Have students fill in squares of a tic-tac-toe grid with numbers no higher than the maximum. Fill a box with slips of paper that range from 1 to the maximum number. When students perform a designated task, let them draw a number. When they draw a number on their grid, they make an X. When they get tic-tac-toe, they earn a reinforcer.	Slot machines: They are programmed to pay off only a certain proportion of times they are played

(continues)

Table 1.4. (continued)

Schedule type	Definition	School example	Real-life example
Fixed interval (e.g., FI 5)	• Provides reinforcement for the *first response* following a fixed duration of time (don't reinforce when the time is up; reinforce after the first desired behavior *after* the time is up) • Often you see a postreinforcement pause followed by a slight increase right before the interval ends (this is called an FI scallop) • Overall shows slow-to-moderate rates of response • Longer intervals usually cause longer postreinforcement pauses and lower overall rates of response	You could make reinforcement available on an FI 2-minute schedule for correct answers on a math worksheet	Getting the mail: It usually comes at the same time each day. You can check it all you want before that time, but it won't be there. The first time you check it after it comes, you get it. Being paid hourly (for every hour you work, you are paid)
Variable interval (e.g., VI 4)	• Tends to produce constant, stable rates of response • Tends to produce low-to-moderate rates of response	Pop quizzes usually result in more consistent study behavior than scheduled quizzes, for instance Seldom applied in systematic ways (because it is hard to determine the maximum VI interval and hard to keep up with the randomized timing)	Fishing: On average, when you fish at the same location, over time you are likely to catch some fish

of these components are overlapping themes. For example, in the section on goal setting we discuss supporting students in developing measurement tools to collect data toward their goal. This would equate to developing the self-monitoring system discussed in Step 2 of self-monitoring interventions. To further demonstrate how all the procedures can be packaged together as one self-management system, we have developed the case study presented here. One purpose of this case study is to demonstrate how teachers can make instructional decisions about how to blend different self-management interventions based on the specific needs of a student. This case study is based on our experiences as classroom teachers using the approaches previously detailed.

SMI Case Study: Nathan

Context

Nathan is a ninth-grade student who is receiving special education services for a diagnosis of ASD. Nathan also has mild intellectual disability. He uses spontaneous verbal language to communicate but benefits from picture cues and other visual supports. Nathan is reading at the second-grade level and enjoys reading or listening to books about animals and space. He receives special education services in a self-contained classroom for students with ASD who require extensive supports. Nathan's special education teacher, Ms. Ferrell, is determined to meet the needs of all her students through instruction that aligns with both their individualized needs (IEP goals) and grade-level standards. Currently, Ms. Ferrell has designed a 2-week unit on outer space. She designed her lessons using state content standards and scientific practices for students in secondary grades. Several of her students (in addition to Nathan) have expressed interest in outer space, and she is excited for the opportunity to provide instruction on this topic.

There are eight students in Nathan's class, and Ms. Ferrell has two instructional aides throughout the day. Based on her knowledge of her students' reading level, she has designed literacy-based science lessons that can be delivered to three small groups for 20 minutes each. Nathan is a member of the first group, along with two other students who have similar reading and listening comprehension skills. One member of the group uses spontaneous speech to voice responses to questions or read aloud with the teacher. Nathan and another girl both primarily point or gesture to indicate a response. Nathan enjoys proximity to both teachers and peers, and he is often distracted in small-group formats. He will often smile and gaze at people instead of attending to work tasks. Sometimes he reaches for others and especially likes to touch the hair or face of the person sitting next to him. Ms. Ferrell (or other adults in the classroom) can easily redirect him by saying, "Show me good working, Nathan," but this prompt does not eliminate the behavior. Ms. Ferrell knows Nathan is interested in the topic of space and wants to help him increase his time on task to maximize his learning. To address Nathan's needs and support access to science learning in her classroom, Ms. Ferrell decides to do two things. First, she will design her lessons using best practices to maximize on-task behaviors, and second, she will teach Nathan to actively manage his own behaviors.

Across the 2-week unit, Ms. Ferrell designs literacy-based science lessons that are engaging and accessible for all her students. By universally designing lessons and preparing materials, and using environmental supports, Ms. Ferrell is able to proactively promote on-task behaviors for all of her students. During their time with her, students engage in literacy-based science lessons meant to provide the background knowledge and context necessary for comprehension of science concepts. First, students read (or listen to) adapted science texts about outer space. Ms. Ferrell adapts grade-level texts to a second-grade reading comprehension level so the students in her class can read along or listen to the story and understand the concepts. To create supported texts, Ms. Ferrell places picture symbols over key vocabulary words and includes high-resolution photographic images next to each page of text.

Ms. Ferrell also develops vocabulary word cards for key science vocabulary in each section of text. Using example/nonexample training, Ms. Ferrell will teach the concepts of these words and model their identification and use throughout instruction. Finally, Ms. Ferrell plans to use systematic response-prompting procedures (a hierarchy of prompts from least intrusive to most intrusive) to teach her students to find answers to comprehension questions in the text. She knows that these visual supports, along with explicit and systematic instructional techniques, will ensure a high rate of active student response and engagement for her students. Now that she has proactively planned her lesson and made materials with the goal of reducing barriers and promoting engagement, it is time to teach Nathan to manage his off-task behaviors. The following sections explain the steps Ms. Ferrell can take to help Nathan set his own goals, monitor his own behaviors, and deliver his own reinforcement.

Goal Setting

To help set and plan goals for Nathan's SMI, Ms. Ferrell helps Nathan complete goal-setting and goal-planning worksheets. Each worksheet has three parts, and Ms. Ferrell uses these worksheets as tools to help Nathan increase awareness of his own strengths and needs, identify worthwhile goals, and plan for the materials and supports he will need during the self-monitoring portion of his intervention. Much of Ms. Ferrell's approach is teacher guided; she uses modeling (including think-aloud modeling) to show Nathan how to respond to each component of the worksheet, and then she gives Nathan a chance to respond on his own. She is careful to use systematic instruction (i.e., constant time delay) and explicit instruction (i.e., example/nonexample procedures) to preteach any terms or concepts that Nathan does not know. Also, she links concepts by reminding Nathan about related responses as he works through the parts of the worksheets. Prior to beginning instruction, Ms. Ferrell considered the components of the worksheets and made adjustments as needed to tailor them to Nathan's specific needs. For example, she chose response options for the worksheets that matched what she knew about Nathan's areas of needs, as well as his interests and strengths. She also included some distractor items to help promote both understanding and engagement. Overall, Ms. Ferrell used the goal-setting phase of Nathan's SMI to promote engagement and build background knowledge to better prepare him for self-monitoring procedures. Nathan's completed worksheets are shown in Figures 1.15 (goal setting) and 1.16 (goal planning).

Before moving on to self-monitoring instruction, Nathan and Ms. Ferrell fill out a behavior contract to identify the reinforcers he will earn when he achieves his goal. Ms. Ferrell shows Nathan his goal-setting worksheet, and they discuss his responses about personal interests. She also gives Nathan a reinforcer inventory that helps them both identify his preference for teacher attention. Together they decide that for each session where he meets his goal, Nathan will earn 2 minutes of one-on-one teacher time with Ms. Ferrell at the end of each 20-minute lesson. They also decide that when Nathan meets his goal of being on task for most of each science lesson for 1 week, he will earn lunch with his teacher. Now that Ms. Ferrell has helped Nathan select and plan his goals, she is ready to begin the steps of a self-monitoring intervention. Within these steps, she will develop a system for monitoring and measuring Nathan's behavior as well as help Nathan determine consequences and rewards.

Self-Monitoring

Next, Ms. Ferrell collects baseline data to better understand the target behaviors Nathan helped identify. She monitors and records Nathan's off-task behaviors during a science lesson and determines he requires a lot of prompts (10 or more, on average) to attend to science lessons. He also inappropriately touches others (touches their hair, reaches for their face) approximately seven times per lesson. Since these are high-frequency behaviors, Ms. Ferrell decides to use a cued monitoring system with intervals of 2 minutes. Next, she develops the materials Nathan will need to monitor his own behavior (see Figure 1.17). With this system, Nathan will respond to a "yes/no" monitoring prompt for each behavior.

Next, Ms. Ferrell is ready to teach Nathan to use his self-monitoring system. To prepare for this training, Ms. Ferrell creates a brief task analysis, or step-by-step breakdown of the steps Nathan will follow when self-monitoring his own behavior. This task analysis includes picture supports or visual cues, and the readability level of the steps matches Nathan's second-grade reading/listening comprehension level. Ms. Ferrell includes picture symbols to promote independent understanding of the steps, and the task analysis is created electronically using GoWorksheet Maker

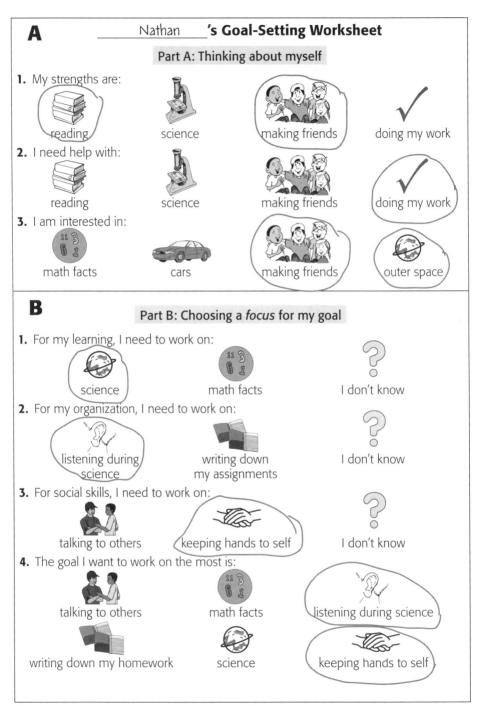

Figure 1.15. Nathan's goal-setting worksheet.

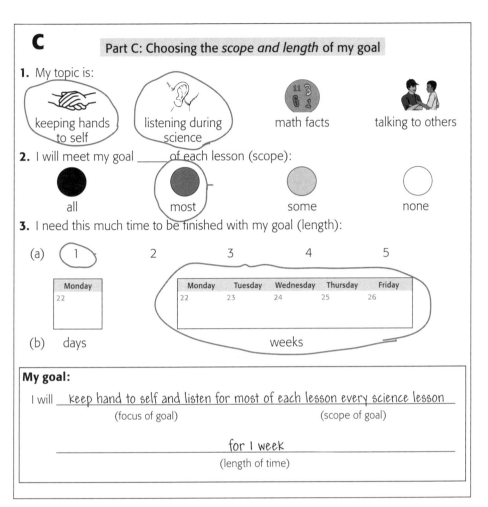

Figure 1.15. *(continued)*

so that Nathan can access supported text-to-speech features (he can voice each step himself, as needed). Ms. Ferrell is careful to write steps that are brief and straightforward. Steps for Nathan's "I am doing my work" behavior are as follows: When the timer dings, (1) *I think about whether I am listening and keeping my hands to myself;* (2) *I decide whether* "I am doing my work" *or* "I am *not* doing my work"; and (3) *I circle the best answer.* Supporting images for the task analysis include an image of a timer, an image of ears and hands, images of a green check mark and a red *X* with a thought bubble, and an image of a pencil or dry-erase marker.

A   _____Nathan_____**'s Goal-Planning Worksheet**

Part A: Materials

1. What materials do I need?

books   calculator   pencil   HIT Timer

2. How will I get my materials?

my teacher   the classroom   other students   someone else

B   **Part B: Steps for achieving my goal**

My goal is to:

Listen and keep my hands to myself during science

To meet my goal:

1st

1. First, I will _____

2nd

2. Next, I will _____

3rd

3. Last, I will _____

Response options for sequencing

Write down if I am meeting my goal
Think about if I am meeting my goal
Get my materials for meeting my goal

Figure 1.16. Nathan's goal-planning worksheet.

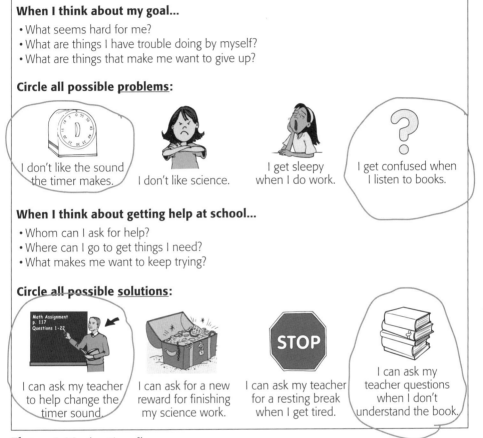

Figure 1.16. *(continued)*

After preparing the task analysis for the self-monitoring process, Ms. Ferrell is ready to teach the concept of the target behavior ("doing my work"). Example/nonexample (or discrimination) training is an effective strategy for teaching students with extensive support needs to identify when a target behavior is or is not occurring. For Nathan, visual supports will be helpful for teaching the concept of the target behavior. To represent the critical features of the target concept, Ms. Ferrell chooses five to seven images that represent both examples of the target behavior and nonexamples of the target behavior. She selects photographs of Nathan looking at the teacher talking and working on tasks. She includes nonexamples of Nathan touching others' hair or faces. Additionally, Ms. Ferrell creates a response option for "example"

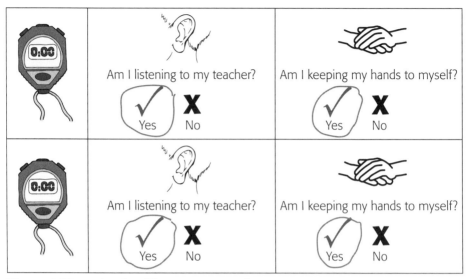

Figure 1.17. Nathan's self-monitoring tool.

and "nonexample" to allow Nathan to receptively label each image accordingly (e.g., a card with a green check mark for "is an example" and a card with a red X for "is *not* an example").

Using the model–lead–test format, Ms. Ferrell teaches the concept of the behavior to Nathan across three rounds. First, she lays the cards down on the table in a line, mixing the order of examples and nonexamples. She conducts a "model" round of instruction by telling Nathan to watch her find examples of "doing your work." She points to each card and immediately holds up the corresponding label (a card with a green check mark for "is an example" or a card with a red X for "is *not* an example"). For example, after pointing to a picture of Nathan looking at the teacher, she says, "This is doing your work! This is on task because you're listening to your teacher." Embedding a brief explanation helps Nathan understand the key features of the target concept. Ms. Ferrell continues labeling and explaining all the cards using brief verbal descriptions and the green check mark/red X response cards. For the next round (the "lead" round), she gives Nathan his own set of green check mark/red X response cards and asks him to label the pictures with her. She mixes up the order of the pictures and proceeds through the same procedures as the "model" round, this time leading or encouraging Nathan to select the correct label for each picture. Finally, she conducts the "test" round by mixing the order of the target cards one more time and instructing Nathan to label each card independently as she touches or points to each card in turn. Ms. Ferrell immediately corrects any errors by showing Nathan the correct label (green check mark or red *X*). She reinforces independent correct responses immediately using specific verbal praise.

Once Nathan has explicitly learned the concept of the target behavior, he is taught the specific steps of the self-monitoring process. Again, using the model–lead–test format, Ms. Ferrell teaches Nathan to follow the steps of the task analysis to track his own target behavior. First, she models use of the task analysis steps by gesturing to each step on the task analysis and succinctly explaining what she is doing at each step. Next, she leads Nathan through the steps of the task analysis. She continues gesturing to each step of the task analysis and provides think-aloud modeling (i.e., succinctly explaining what she is doing) as needed. Finally, she tests Nathan by instructing him to follow the steps of the task analysis independently. To provide additional instruction when needed, she is prepared to use least-to-most prompting to provide supports if Nathan is unsure what to do at each step or makes an error. For example, if Nathan does not react when the buzzer beeps, a first-level prompt could be to point or gesture to the task analysis as a cue to follow the steps. If Nathan still does not initiate the steps of the task analysis, Ms. Ferrell provides Nathan with a verbal cue, like, "Remember, your first step is ____." If Nathan still does not initiate the steps of the task analysis, she provides a model prompt of completing the first step. She continues this hierarchy, as needed, across the steps of the self-monitoring task analysis.

After training, Ms. Ferrell implements the self-monitoring system and teaches an instructional aide to confirm that Nathan is answering the monitoring prompts independently and accurately. If he makes an error with his recording or accuracy of recording, the aide administers error correction procedures by pointing out the mistake and modeling the correct behavior. Periodically, Ms. Ferrell collects follow-up data of her own on Nathan's "doing his work" behavior. She graphs the data and highlights the agreed-upon reinforcement criterion of "most" of the time (which she has defined as 80% of the time on task). Now Nathan is ready to learn how to consider his own progress and determine whether he has earned his reinforcement.

Self-Reinforcement

During every science lesson, Nathan monitors and evaluates his target behavior. Ms. Ferrell teaches Nathan to look at his daily data and determine whether it is above or below the highlighted line. Nathan is taught to look for daily progress and progress over time. If he meets his daily criterion of being "mostly" on task (a data point on or above the highlighted line), he earns 2 minutes of "teacher time." When he sees 5 data points on or above the highlighted line, he earns lunch with the teacher. Ms. Ferrell asks him to self-evaluate both his daily and weekly goals every session. He indicates with a "yes/no" response card whether he met his daily goal and earned 2 minutes of teacher time and met his weekly goal and earned lunch with his teacher. Finally, to promote maintenance of the skills over time, Ms. Ferrell fades

Nathan's first schedule of reinforcement (FR1, or fixed ratio #1). Instead of reinforcing his progress after every lesson, she changes the criterion to reinforce him after every other lesson. After Nathan maintains his on-task behaviors over another week at this new intermittent reinforcement schedule (FR2), Ms. Ferrell begins fading his self-monitoring system. Instead of checking his progress every 2 minutes, Nathan is taught to check his progress every 4 minutes. With these new criteria in place, Nathan continues to demonstrate on-task behaviors during his science lesson.

PART TWO Cognitive Behavior Interventions

What Are Cognitive Behavior Interventions?

As discussed in the introduction, there are a variety of approaches besides self-management that combine cognitive and behavioral modification techniques. These cognitive behavior interventions (CBIs) are a notoriously broad, often loosely connected group of tools designed to repair the faulty thinking processes and/or emotional responses that so often lead to problematic behavior and poor social competence. These methods fall on a broad continuum, from formal approaches to psychotherapy to teacher-created programs to commercially available curricula. They have commonality in that they promote active problem solving, self-reflection and evaluation, and emotional recognition, among other cognitive skills. Similarly, these methods are generally packaged with instructional and behavioral approaches, including direct skill instruction, positive reinforcement, modeling, and behavioral rehearsals.

CBI and ASD

Currently, the majority of the research on CBI for students with ASD is centered on multicomponent programs, and these programs are often group-instructional interventions. There is also some support for other problem-solving and self-evaluation approaches as stand-alone tools, though more research is needed in these areas. These CBI techniques are used primarily to support students with high-functioning ASD (HFASD) in social skill acquisition/performance and in reductions of antisocial behaviors. They also seem to have some efficacy in reducing the symptoms of anxiety and depression so often experienced by students with HFASD. The rest of this guide focuses on providing an overview of these multicomponent programs and specific implementation considerations. This section of the guide closes with a case study profiling an instructional group using CBI approaches.

Multicomponent CBI Programs

Overview

There are many instructional interventions that use both cognitive and behavioral modification techniques to improve social skill and social problem-solving outcomes for students with ASD. These approaches are based on cognitive behavior therapy (CBT), which is a formal approach to psychotherapy based on the cognitive model. While CBT takes many forms, it is generally centered on the idea that social and behavioral problems arise from faulty or inaccurate thinking (Mennuti, Freeman, & Christner, 2006). These thinking inaccuracies include things like misinterpreting the seriousness of a situation, misunderstanding someone's intentions, misidentifying emotions, or engaging in overly rigid thinking. It is easy to see how these inaccuracies can in turn cause a host of social and behavioral difficulties. CBT is one of the most widely researched types of psychotherapy and has demonstrated effectiveness in treating a variety of disorders and issues, including depression, stress and anxiety, social withdrawal, anger and aggression, chronic pain, and personality difficulties (Hofmann, Asnaani, Vonk, Sawyer, & Fang, 2012).

Formal approaches to CBT have recently been calibrated for students with ASD. These approaches are often structured, group treatment programs targeting social understanding and problem solving. Many of these programs are available commercially, including the strand of social thinking curricula (Winner, 2005; e.g., *Think Social!, Superflex . . . A Superhero Social Thinking Curriculum, We Thinkers, Unthinkables,* etc.) and other similar curricula (e.g., *The Hidden Curriculum for Understanding Unstated Rules in Social Situations for Adolescents and Young Adults, Navigating the Social World*). Others are developed by retrofitting CBT models to meet the needs of learners with ASD. These include approaches like Program for the Education and Enrichment of Relational Skills (PEERS; Laugeson, Frankel, Gantman, Dillon, & Mogil, 2012) and Multimodal Anxiety and Social Skills Intervention (MASSI; White et al., 2013). MASSI, PEERS, and other similar programs have substantial research to support their implementation, so much so that multicomponent CBI programs are now listed as an evidence-based practice by both the National Professional Development Center on Autism Spectrum Disorder (NCPD-ASD) and the National Autism Center's National Standards Project. These programs are designed to improve the underlying cognitive processes that so often lead to the social difficulties experienced by many individuals with ASD. By emphasizing skill acquisition *and* social understanding and problem solving, these programs are specifically targeting the executive functioning, emotional regulation, and theory-of-mind deficits that are well documented for individuals with ASD (see Table 2.1).

Table 2.1. Definitions of Key Cognitive Processes

Cognitive process	Definition	Resulting social difficulties
Executive functioning	Umbrella term that refers to the processes one uses to self-regulate, manage working memory effectively, plan ahead, and maintain flexibility (Liss et al., 2001)	Reciprocal conversations, appropriate emotional responses, perseverative interests and thoughts, stimulus overselectivity, rigidity of thinking and acting
Theory of mind	The mental processes of perspective taking and accurately interpreting the emotions and intentions of others (Lacava, Golan, Baron-Cohen, & Smith Myles, 2007)	Empathy, emotional recognition, appropriate emotional responses
Emotional regulation	The mental processes that assist in self-control and self-awareness (Berkovits, Eisenhower, & Blachar, 2017)	Emotional recognition, emotional responses, behavioral control, understanding and interpreting nuanced emotions in self and others

Note. These mental processes are not mutually exclusive. They often confound social competence in complex and overlapping ways for students with ASD.

These programs have great promise for students with autism. However, the commercially available programs can be expensive, and while many of them are based on sound theoretical foundations, most of them have not been vetted by rigorous scientific investigation. The programs that have been carefully vetted by researchers are complex and often require specific training or credentialing (e.g., PEERS) or knowledge of psychotherapy to implement successfully. However, these programs do have some commonalities that we believe teachers could use with fidelity to address the social deficits of individuals with ASD. Namely, these programs often rely on *specific skill instruction, problematic thinking habits, behavioral rehearsal and feedback activities,* and *visual supports and other scaffolds* (National Autism Center, 2015) to achieve improvements in social skill performance and reductions in antisocial behavior. While presenting the specific implementation steps for each component of these CBI programs is not practical in this guide (and frankly is redundant given what is available in other manual-like commercially available programs), it is our intent to describe each of these steps in sufficient detail that practitioners can develop similar programs with similar features or can supplement their current programs to include CBI approaches.

Specific Skill Instruction

Specific skill instruction is integral to the success of the group or individual program. These types of programs often rely on experiential learning activities and can often revolve around particular problems (either case study problems or students' actual lived experiences). The reason this skill instruction step is so important is because we know that students who do not have good background knowledge (e.g., foundation information or skills relevant to the content being taught) learn very little from experiential learning activities (see Kirschner, Sweller, & Clark, 2006). The purpose of this step is to explicitly teach specific skills that students do not fully understand so they can apply these skills during the problem-solving and cognitive restructuring activities that will follow this skill instruction. Otherwise, students have little hope of acquiring these skills through experience alone. This step involves formal instruction about individually relevant skills. This generally includes instruction regarding emotion recognition, coping actions or activities, and specific social skills, as well as information about the challenges faced by individuals with similar skills and deficits. Let us explore each of these topics briefly.

Instruction will likely need to occur relative to *feelings and emotions.* This instruction can include how to identify one's own specific emotions and how to identify specific emotions in others. When learning to identify emotions in themselves, students often learn to associate certain physical symptoms and certain contextual variables with specific emotions. This seems particularly necessary with similar or nuanced emotions. For example, an accelerated heart rate and sweaty palms could mean excitement, fear, and/or nervousness. To determine exactly how they are feeling, students can briefly attend to what is happening around them. Are they getting ready to ride a rollercoaster or talk to a potential romantic partner? Well then, they might be experiencing excitement. If, however, they are getting ready to talk in front of a large group, they might be feeling the same physical symptoms, but experiencing the emotion of fear or nervousness. These nuances are important, as the acceptable behaviors related to excitement and fear are completely different. Similarly, the way we might seek to cope with these emotions is also different. Specific instruction on recognizing emotions in oneself can be accomplished through direct instruction on the distinct types of emotions, modeling (via video and in-vivo exemplars), and example/nonexample training.

Accurately interpreting the emotions of others is also a necessary skill to teach explicitly to many students with HFASD. Similar to the process of recog-

64

nizing specific emotions in themselves, students are taught to look for physical and contextual clues that might inform them about how other people are feeling. These physical clues can include body language and facial expressions. It is well documented that students with HFASD often attend to the wrong physical clues when interacting with others. For example, they might be looking at the person's face when interacting with him or her but not at the specific areas of the face where facial expressions are demonstrated (i.e., the eyes and mouth). Similarly, students with HFASD might focus on specific physical clues but ignore context. Students can be taught using a variety of instructional approaches to attend to both the contextual environment and the individual to make an inference about what the other person is feeling. They can also be taught specific, appropriate responses to the emotions of others.

Besides instruction on emotional recognition, it can be helpful to provide specific instruction about how to respond to specific emotions. This generally involves instruction on specific *coping strategies*. Students with HFASD can be easily overwhelmed by intense emotions and often need direct adult/teacher involvement to respond appropriately to daily emotions such as anger, embarrassment, frustration, annoyance, and excitement. Instruction on coping strategies should include specific identification of different coping strategies (e.g., taking deep breaths, taking a break, exercising), as well as specific instruction on aligning coping strategies with specific emotions. Once students understand specific coping strategies, they can make individualized plans to deploy them when faced with intense emotions. These coping plans can be formalized in writing and used as a priming tool before difficult activities or interactions, or as a prompt when students are not responding appropriately to intense emotions.

In addition to emotional recognition and responses to intense emotions, students might need to be taught specific social skills. In this context, *social skills* refers to the discrete skills that make up successful social interactions. These skills include making greetings and social initiations, complimenting others, asking and answering questions, demonstrating topic maintenance, and listening and responding. It is often incorrectly assumed that students with HFASD do not need specific skill instruction, but rather need only instruction on performing social skills successfully. Not all students will need instruction on all social skills, and conducting initial assessments can help you determine which skills you should focus on for particular students. We encourage you to consult the book in this series titled *Social Skills and Social Interactions* (Stichter & Conroy, 2018). This book has valuable guidelines on specific social skill assessments to help you plan which skills to target, and provides reasonable instructional approaches to teaching specific social skills.

Finally, it is not uncommon for these types of approaches to attempt to teach students something about themselves by giving them *information on HFASD*, anxiety, and social interactions (see White et al., 2013). This often includes specific information about common social deficits associated with ASD and how similar individuals have overcome these deficits. Students with HFASD often do not see how their behavior affects the way others treat them. They might realize that people are excluding them or not associating with them, but they might not realize why this is occurring. Frank discussions about the social characteristics of individuals with ASD or the effects of anxiety on social interactions can help them understand why peers are often alienated by their behavior. Similarly, it can help them to know that other people have similar experiences and have made progress addressing these behaviors in this way.

Addressing Problematic Thinking Habits

One of the aims of multicomponent CBI programs is to specifically target the thinking inaccuracies that perpetuate problematic social behaviors. This is generally done by identifying particularly problematic ways of thinking and providing alternative ways of thinking, which can be accomplished by (a) naming specific ways of thinking that create problems, (b) providing instruction on why this way of thinking is problematic, and (c) developing a visual representation of the thinking problem. For example, one problematic way of thinking is called *catastrophizing*. This way of thinking blows things way out of proportion, so that things that are not really that big a deal (e.g., being a few minutes late, forgetting your pencil) become consuming and prevent an individual from moving on from minor setbacks. Many students could benefit from brief and direct instruction about this way of thinking and the problems it causes. Similarly, this could be paired with a visual cue that represents this problematic way of thinking and used to remind or prompt students to be cautious of thinking this way. Many of the packaged curricula have developed useful activities and routines around these problematic ways of thinking. Other examples of potentially difficult ways of thinking include *minimizing* (thinking of something as less important than it is), *jumping to conclusions* (assuming you know why someone acted as he or she did), and *all or nothing* (something undertaken must be done exactly perfectly or not at all). To be clear, it is not certain to what degree we can actually change the thinking processes of students with ASD. These processes are internal to their cognition and as such are unmeasurable. However, we can measure their social actions and inactions, which are reasonably tied to these thinking processes. We can also teach them to identify and define these types of potential roadblocks so they can recognize them in their own thinking and work to overcome them.

Behavioral Rehearsals and Feedback Routines

Specific opportunities to perform social interaction skills and mechanisms for delivering specific and time-sensitive feedback are also frequently featured in the multicomponent CBI programs. Behavioral rehearsals generally involve role-playing scenarios, case examples, and/or videotaped skill demonstrations. The purpose of these behavioral rehearsals is to give students opportunities to practice specific social skills in a safe and supportive environment. These rehearsals can occur in group or individual treatments. A few things to keep in mind when developing opportunities for behavioral rehearsals include (a) starting with scripted or structured scenarios, (b) providing prompts when needed, and (c) moving eventually to more spontaneous scenarios that mimic naturally occurring social interactions. For example, early in the CBI program, students might have specific scripts or scenarios prewritten by the teacher; part of the program would have them act out these scenarios in formal role-play situations. As students make progress through the program, these rehearsals might involve playing a board game with friends or engaging in other activities that more closely mimic naturally occurring social interactions.

Similarly, these programs also feature specific mechanisms for delivering feedback to students. These feedback routines are designed to provide specific input on the quality of the student's social interactions and can include formal ratings of specific behaviors and qualitative feedback about specific aspects of the skill performance. These feedback routines should be structured and should also look for ways to involve students in self-evaluating their performance.

One type of qualitative, structured feedback often used in these types of programs is video feedback (Maione & Mirenda, 2006; Thiemann & Goldstein, 2001). *Video feedback* involves videotaped behavioral rehearsals and formal self-evaluation routines to improve social competence and social problem solving. Video feedback can be a powerful tool for complex social behaviors. The benefit of the video clips is that instructors can pause and rewind the video. This control over the medium allows for problem-solving conversations about specific, often complex behaviors (such as those involving body language, voice tone and volume, and facial expressions) and the emotional and environmental variables that maintain them. Similarly, students can evaluate their performance using specific rating or recording tools and set goals for future behavior, as well as see positive examples of themselves performing specific behaviors. When using video feedback, ensure that students have targeted evaluation materials and can rate or evaluate specific behaviors contained within the video. Also, make sure to have video clips that demonstrate some desired behaviors. Students who consistently watch only negative examples of their behavior may be unmotivated or uninterested in continuing these types of problem-solving approaches. Also, the video-modeling literature is clear that students can benefit greatly from seeing positive examples of their own behavior. See Figure 2.1 for an example of a video feedback self-evaluation form.

Another way that video feedback can work is to have students watch video exemplars culled from television episodes, movies, or other video sources. The

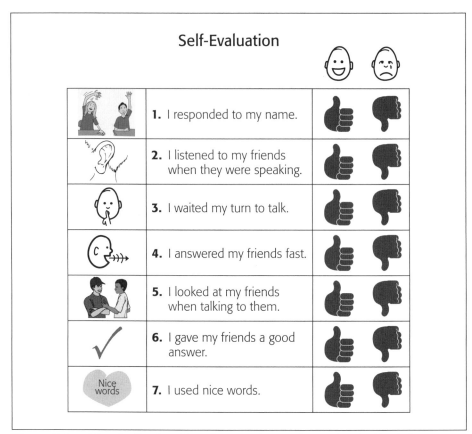

Figure 2.1. Video feedback self-evaluation form. This video feedback form was used by an elementary student to rate his question-answering behavior during game play.

target students will not be the subjects of these videos, but they can rate the behavior of the individuals in the videos using a rating scale or other type of structured evaluation (e.g., rubrics, short answer). Again, the value here is that students can view the video, evaluate the behaviors of interest, and then debrief with an adult, rewatching relevant sections of the clip as needed. Given how ubiquitous video technology has become, thanks to the advances made in mobile device technology, creating and viewing brief video clips is now easier than ever before. In our opinion, this practice represents an underutilized CBI tool that both practitioners and researchers should continue to explore.

Students may also benefit from quantitative feedback where "experts" (teachers, aides, and others) provide immediate ratings of student behaviors across several variables of interest (e.g., voice tone and volume, body language, specific social skills). This feedback can then be reviewed by the teacher and students.

Similarly, as students become more familiar with these rating systems, they can use them to rate their own behavior during video feedback routines or after social activities. Giving students a quantitative score following these rehearsals can also allow adult facilitators to track progress over time, display progress for students, and measure gains in naturally occurring social situations. See Figure 2.2 for an example of a rating rubric.

Social Skills Rubric

Student Name: _____   Activity: _____

Skill	1	2	3	4
Greeting	Greeting did not occur or was not socially acceptable.	Greeting occurred but was too scripted or formal. Greeting did not feel natural.	Greeting was acceptable. Natural and age appropriate.	Greeting was excellent. Greeting contained BOTH appropriate gestures and vocalizations.
Conversation	Back-and-forth conversation did not occur or was inappropriate.	Conversation was one-sided. (or) Conversation was mostly questions.	Conversation during game play was good.	Conversation was excellent, with more than 3 reciprocal exchanges. Contained both questions and replies.
Body Language	Body language was inappropriate.	Body language did not fit the situation, too formal or rigid. Staring or awkward postures.	Body language during game play was good.	Body language was excellent. Looked at peers when talking. Smiled when necessary.
Voice Volume/Tone	Voice was too loud for the situation or voice tone was upsetting to others.	Voice tone or volume was inconsistent, fluctuated too much for the situation.	Voice tone and volume were BOTH good throughout the activity.	Voice tone and voice volume were excellent. Fluctuations occurred where appropriate.

Rubric Total Score: _____   *Scores higher than 12 = 👌

Figure 2.2. Rating rubric used after behavioral rehearsals for middle school students with HFASD.

Visual Supports and Other Scaffolds

The programs discussed here also often feature specific visual supports that are woven throughout the instructional activities and ideally transferred to naturally occurring social situations. These visual supports scaffold the processes of self-evaluation and self-reflection and can also help students predict likely outcomes of their behavior. These supports are generally taught within the context of the CBI program and then transitioned to broad usage across the students' daily activities.

Two visual scaffolds that can enhance the problem-solving capabilities of students with ASD are visual scales and consequence maps. *Visual scales* are based on *The Incredible 5-Point Scale* (Buron & Curtis, 2003), a teacher-created visual scaffold that supports a variety of self-evaluation and self-reflection behaviors for students with ASD. Visual scales represent specific behaviors and problem-solving scenarios through numeric scales (generally 1–5 or 1–10). Much in the same way that a visual timer displays the abstract concept of lapsing time, these scales represent distinct levels of emotions, thinking, and behavior that might not be clear to individuals with ASD. They often address specific nuances of behavior and actions that are easily overlooked by these individuals. These scales are often color coded to reflect different levels of behaving or functioning (e.g., green for *okay* or *good*, yellow for *caution*, red for *danger*). The utility of these scales seems to be in their broad application and the self-evaluation and -reflection routines that can be established around these scales. These scales can be established around a variety of behaviors and thinking processes. They can be used to evaluate voice volume, reflect on feelings and emotions, determine the relative importance of a problem or situation, and establish social norms or rules. See Figure 2.3 for examples of visual scales.

These are just examples of the broad applicability that these visual scales have for students with ASD. When using these scales, first identify the behaviors, emotions, or thinking processes that are currently problematic for specific students. Then, break these variables of interest into small steps or actions that are observable and easily identifiable to the students. Whenever possible, these supports should be cocreated with the students in order to arrive at a scale that is meaningful to them. Next, associate colors and numbers with the scale. You can also associate specific actions with each level of the scale. These actions can then be used to alert students to possible coping strategies or behaviors that they can engage in to move to a more desirable level of the scale. These scales can be used before or after behavioral rehearsals and during daily situations. As the creators of the tool caution, this is a teaching tool that should be used to help students problem solve and reflect on their behavior or emotions.

Consequence maps, sometimes called *contingency maps* (Simpson & Tobin, 2012), are a unique problem-solving intervention that seeks to connect specific

1

5	I am yelling! I need a break.	
4	I am getting too loud!	
3	I am happy. I am using my classroom voice.	
2	I am too quiet. My friends and teachers cannot hear what I am saying.	
1	I am not responding to my friends and teachers. This makes them sad.	

2

How Big Is My Problem?

Scale	1–2	3–4	5–6	7	8–9	10
Size of problem	Glitch	Little problem	Medium problem	Big problem	Gigantic problem	Emergency
Do I need help?	You do not need help. You can find a solution to this problem yourself.	You do not need help. You can find a solution to this problem yourself.	You may need a little help from an adult or you could solve this problem yourself.	You are going to need some help from an adult.	You are going to need some help from an adult.	Get help immediately.
Examples	You stubbed your toe. Someone bumps into you in the hall-way. You don't know what a word means in your book. You lost a game. Someone is not taking turns. You have made a mess.	You are thirsty. You need to use the restroom. Someone is annoying you. You have homework assigned in class. You lose a game.	Someone says something you do not like. You are afraid. You need help on a math problem. You don't understand the directions for an assignment.	Someone is mean to you or takes something that is yours. A minor accident. You need help calming down.	You are lost. Someone is hurting you or you feel like hitting, kicking, or punching. You feel like throwing or breaking things. Someone is bullying you.	Someone is hurt and needs to go to the hospital. Car accident. Fire.

(continues)

Figure 2.3. Examples of visual scales: (1) represents a visual scale for emotion recognition; (2) represents a problem-solving visual scale to determine how big a problem really is.

Scale	1-2	3-4	5-6	7	8-9	10
Size of problem	Glitch	Little problem	Medium problem	Big problem	Gigantic problem	Emergency
School strategy	Take a deep breath. Count to 10. Use a dictionary. Clean up your mess.	Take a deep breath. Ask to switch seats. Ask to get a drink. Use the restroom at the next break. Write your homework down in your planner so you can remember. Tell your friend "good game" and that you'll beat him/her next time.	Ask a friend for help. Ask the teacher to reexplain the assignment. Tell the person to leave you alone.	Ask for your item to be returned. Explain to the teacher that someone has something that is yours, in private. Ask for a break. Tell your parents after school.	Find an adult. Get away from other people by going to a safe place.	Get an adult. Call 911. Use help button on the wall in the classroom. Pull fire alarm.

Figure 2.3. *(continued)*

behaviors to likely outcomes. As discussed earlier, students with ASD often have a difficult time connecting their behaviors to the social outcomes they experience. Consequence maps are designed to visually represent the cause-and-effect link between specific behaviors or emotions and logical consequences, as well as provide the context for an adult-led problem-solving discussion. When used in a CBI program, these tools can help students connect their behavior to likely outcomes and can also help them consider ways to avoid less desirable consequences (see Figure 2.4).

Consequence maps are also used outside of CBI programs for naturally occurring situations. Regardless of whether you are using them as a teaching tool within a CBI program or as a visual support as part of a larger behavior modification package, consequence maps generally consist of one specific antecedent and two (or more) "behavior tracks." The antecedent should represent the most likely trigger for the behavior and could include a task demand, such as "math time"; an environmental trigger, such as "end of recess" or "lunchtime in the cafeteria"; and/or an emotional trigger, such as "feeling frustrated." The two behavioral tracks represent possible student responses to the antecedent. One track should represent a positive or desired response, and the other track should represent an undesired or problematic response. It can be helpful to color code the tracks, us-

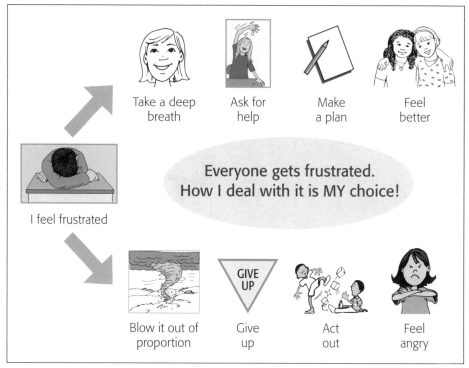

Figure 2.4. Example of a consequence map used to connect specific feelings to possible outcomes.

ing a positive color (e.g., green for "go," the student's favorite color) for the desired track and a negative color (e.g., red for "stop," the student's least favorite color) for the undesired track. Each track should end with a logical consequence. For the positive track, this should represent forms of positive reinforcement for the target student, while the undesired track should end in a naturally occurring punishing consequence, such as the loss of privileges or lack of access to reinforcement. See Figure 2.5 for a sample consequence map.

The problem-solving discussion should be a brief priming exercise, immediately prior to the triggering antecedent. (If the antecedent is an emotional state, then review the consequence map on a specific schedule, such as every morning or afternoon.) Start by simply reading through the consequence map; read the negative track first, and end by reading the positive track. Focus carefully on each of the consequences, and clearly explain the likely outcomes of the behaviors in each track. End the priming exercise by asking students which track they would like to maintain. Keep the consequence map visible, and if students start demonstrating behaviors represented by the negative track, ask them to self-evaluate

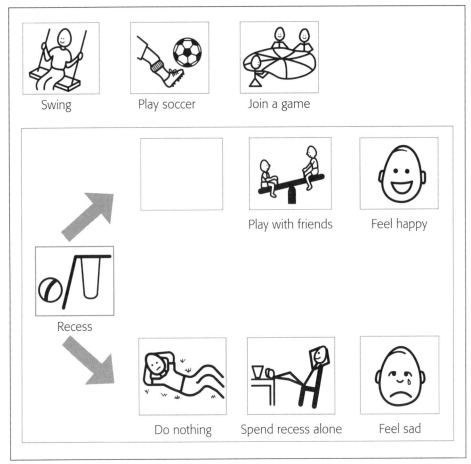

Figure 2.5. Example of a consequence map.

by asking them to identify their current track. Remind them of the consequences of their actions if they continue down this track, and help them identify actions that would get them back on the right track. This type of intervention is ideal for behaviors that have more distal consequences, are already a part of the student's behavioral repertoire, and have clearly identifiable triggers. Once the behavior starts to move in the desired direction, you can fade to more generalizable reinforcers, such as social praise, or increase the criteria needed for reinforcement. Consequence maps are easy to create and can be efficiently delivered and managed. They help students predict the outcomes of their behavior and help them structure their thinking and plan ahead. In this way, consequence maps can be powerful tools, especially when paired with powerful reinforcers.

Last Thoughts

The components of CBI programs outlined here represent an attempt to demystify these often-complex instructional programs. Many good manuals exist (e.g., see *CBT for Children and Adolescents with High-Functioning Autism Spectrum Disorders*; Scarpa, White, & Attwood, 2013) for individuals wishing to implement these approaches, and many commercial products hold a good deal of promise. Also, it is important to note that many CBI programs also recommend training parents, providing opportunities for skill practice and generalization across environments, and having participants complete homework assignments designed to test these skills in the real world. Our purpose in highlighting the elements described here is that we believe teachers can implement these types of programs within the school day and can use these types of approaches to improve outcomes for students with ASD. We also believe that many of the problem-solving approaches outlined can be detached from a larger CBI program and used as stand-alone tools to address and practice prosocial behavior. In fact, some research supports using video feedback (Thiemann & Goldstein, 2001), behavioral rehearsals (McGee, Krantz, & McClannahan, 1984), and consequence maps (Tobin & Simpson, 2012) as components of treatment packages to improve student behavior. To illustrate how teachers can, in fact, use these types of multicomponent programs to facilitate social skills, we present the following case study of a social skills program. This case was built on one of the author's personal experiences as a middle school teacher (see Crutchfield, Weber, & Simpson, 2013) and other lived accounts of classroom teachers around the country.

CBI Case Study: Mr. Hill's Seventh-Grade Homeroom

Overview and Program Planning

Jeff Hill is a middle school special education teacher. His primary caseload consists of students with ASD. He is currently concerned about several of his students who are receiving their special education services in general education settings. These students are mostly getting good grades and making progress academically. However, they are having a difficult time fitting in with their peers (especially during lunch and physical education class) and are also demonstrating some consistent behavioral difficulties in the classroom that have resulted in office referrals and detentions. Through direct observations and discussions with classroom teachers and support staff, Mr. Hill has begun to see a pattern in the challenges faced by these students. They have a difficult time moving past setbacks; even little things like forgetting a pencil or being told to find their seat can sometimes lead to extreme behavioral problems. They also lack certain social skills and somehow manage to always say the wrong things at the wrong time. Mr. Hill sees the potential in these students, but knows that despite their relative academic success, they will likely be unsuccessful in high school and beyond because of these difficulties.

Determined to do something about the situation, Mr. Hill decides he wants to try to address these deficits through a group instructional intervention with individualized scaffolds and supports. He consults some experts, including the district behavior specialist, the school psychologist, and the speech–language pathologist. Together they come up with a plan to address these deficits and improve the social and behavioral outcomes of these students. The plan consists of finding a time to conduct a 25- to 30-minute social skills group two times a week, conducting brief assessments to identify group and individual targets, and designing instructional activities and individual scaffolds.

Finding a time to conduct this training during school hours was the first challenge to overcome. This might seem like a trivial challenge, but Mr. Hill's students were across grade bands and had vastly different schedules. Mr. Hill and his colleagues were hesitant to pull students out of class. Removing students from classes they were doing well in meant fewer opportunities for them to experience success and build expertise. Similarly, removing them from classes that they were doing poorly in risked loss of valuable instructional time. Further, the electives and study skills classes that the students attended afforded valuable, naturally occurring social opportunities and specific strategy instruction, respectively. The two choices Mr. Hill considered were homeroom and lunch. Initially, he thought a lunch group might work. He planned to reach out to area restaurants and ask for gift card donations to some lunch spots that were popular with his students. He could pick up lunch from these special places to provide incentive for attendance and participation, and conduct the training activities as students were eating. However, he finally decided on homeroom. At Mr. Hill's school, all students, regardless of grade bands, spent the first 25 minutes of every day in a homeroom. Here teachers took attendance and reviewed a citizenship curriculum that was part of the school's positive behavior support plan. This afforded Mr. Hill a perfect window of time for his instructional group.

Next, he needed to identify some specific skills to address. He knew what areas the students generally struggled in, but he wanted to identify some concrete skill deficits to address through the program. To do this he conducted several structured observations. He conducted these observations during times that the students in the program were participating in naturally occurring social opportunities. This was mainly in the lunchroom, during group activities in class, and during physical education. During these observations, Mr. Hill used an informal assessment technique called a discrepancy analysis. A *discrepancy analysis* involves attending to same-age peers without ASD and the target students with ASD within the same context. During these observations, Mr. Hill noticed the social skills that the peers were exhibiting and the ways in which they navigated their social environment. He would list the behaviors that these peers were demonstrating. Then he would attend to the students with HFASD and notice the behaviors they were exhibiting. He would subsequently list these behaviors. Later he would compare the two lists and identify social behaviors that the peers were demonstrating that the students with ASD were not demonstrating. He also was able to identify socially awkward or difficult behaviors that the students with ASD were exhibiting that the peers did not demonstrate. Mr. Hill also talked to classroom teachers, related service providers, and the students themselves, and completed an informal rating scale for each student to identify areas of strength and weakness. After conducting his observations and discussions, Mr. Hill identified eight skills that he wanted to address in his homeroom instructional program. These skills included six social skills and two thinking skills (see Table 2.2).

Now that Mr. Hill had overcome the first few obstacles, he was ready to tackle the instructional design of the 30-minute program. He decided on the following schedule for his homeroom, building in 5 minutes of buffer time for transitions between activities and arrival and departure routines. Since there were eight skills in total and the class met two times a week for 10 weeks, Mr. Hill addressed one skill per week and had a culminating project that lasted the final 2 weeks. Mr. Hill developed two schedules for the 30-minute instructional program: one schedule for the introduction of a new skill and one schedule for rehearsal and feedback of the skill (see Table 2.3). Let us look at the each one of these components to get a sense of how Mr. Hill carried out this CBI program.

Skill Introduction

Skill Priming

When introducing a new skill, Mr. Hill provided students with a brief priming activity to orient them to the skill. There were six students participating in the CBI program, so Mr. Hill arranged them into two groups of three. Once the students arrived, he gave them a 2-minute warning before the session would begin. He displayed a visual

Table 2.2. Thinking Skills and Social Skills Identified by Mr. Hill

Thinking skills	Social skills
Moving past mistakes	Social initiations
Letting emotions decide	Listening and responding
	Reciprocal conversations
	Body language
	Voice tone and volume
	Complimenting others

Table 2.3. Schedule for Skill Introductions and Skill Rehearsals

Skill introduction – Tuesdays	Schedule
Skill priming	7:30–7:35
Skill instruction	7:35–7:45
Guided problem solving	7:45–7:55
Skill rehearsal – Thursdays	**Schedule**
Skill priming	7:30–7:35
Skit development	7:35–7:45
Behavioral rehearsal and feedback	7:45–7:55

timer to help cue the students. Once the timer sounded, the students would transition to their tables. If it was a social skill, Mr. Hill developed a rubric in student-friendly language that demonstrated various levels of the skill (bad, okay, and good); if the skill was a thinking skill, he developed a visual scale of the skill, demonstrating different levels of this type of thinking. The students were told to review the materials and talk among themselves about the skill. Mr. Hill visited each group for about two minutes, facilitating conversation about the skill, providing examples or nonexamples of the skill in question, and answering any queries that arose from the group.

Skill Instruction

After the priming exercise, Mr. Hill began a brief instructional routine about the skill. This instructional activity included a brief rationale in which he provided students with reasons why this skill was important and how mastering this skill could lead to improvements in their well-being. This rationale lasted approximately two minutes. After providing the rationale, Mr. Hill called the students' attention to the visual supports (e.g., rubric, visual scale) and reviewed with them the different levels and nuances of the skill. This instruction was clipped and specific. In this instruction, Mr. Hill would focus on the two extremes of the rubric (or the visual scale) and give the students specific things to do and specific things to avoid. These were synthesized as "tips on _____," and the students were provided with a visual with these tips. This lasted about five minutes. For the last two minutes or so of the instructional time, Mr. Hill took questions about the skill from the students. Figure 2.6 presents sample rubrics for the priming and instructional activities.

Guided Problem Solving

The final step of the skill instruction involved video-based problem-solving activities. In these activities, the students watched two or three short video clips. These video

Complimenting Rubric		
BAD	**OK**	**GOOD**
• Sarcastic compliment • Genuine compliment about someone's body • Rude or ironic compliment	• Compliment is too generic • Complimenting someone just so they compliment you • Complimenting at weird times	• Compliment is genuine and relevant • Said with a smile • Said sincerely

Social Initiations		
BAD	**OK**	**GOOD**
• Ignoring friends and acquaintances when you see them • Hugging or other touch that is too personal	• Too scripted or formal ("Hello, how are you doing this afternoon?")	• Eager and pleasant • Appropriate gesture and vocalization • Age appropriate

Figure 2.6. Examples of student rubrics for the priming and instructional activities.

clips were collected by Mr. Hill from two sources: popular TV shows that featured a variety of social skills and deficits (e.g., *Seinfeld*, *Big Bang Theory*, *Frasier*, *iCarly*) and video clips from the students' actual behavioral rehearsals (discussed later in this case study). The students were told that they were going to watch a video clip of the skill in question and that they should be ready to use either the rubric or the visual scale to evaluate the performance of the skill in the clip. The clip (usually 30–45 seconds in length) showed the full context of the skill in question and required the students to attend carefully to locate the skill within the larger context of the interaction. The clip was watched twice, with 30 seconds of think time between viewings. After the students evaluated the clip individually, they shared their ratings with their groups and then with the larger class. Mr. Hill provided feedback on their ratings and corrected any errors.

Skill Rehearsals

Skill Priming

Because time had elapsed since the students' initial engagement with the skill, Mr. Hill wanted to reorient the students to the skill in question. This proceeded in much the same way as the initial priming that occurred during the skill introduction and subsequent instruction. Students were provided with the visual supports and asked to recall what the group had discussed relative to that skill in the prior meeting.

Mr. Hill divided his time between the two groups and answered any remaining questions.

Skit Development

With a good background on the skill in question, students began to develop a brief (1–2 minutes) social skit that demonstrated this skill. They worked from a script stem that Mr. Hill developed to structure the skit (see Figure 2.7). All students were required to participate in the skit and to have a speaking part. To increase interest and engagement, Mr. Hill brought in some props (e.g., sunglasses, hats, sports equipment, video game controllers) to help the skits be more convincing and seem like a true social performance. Students were allowed to choose the context of the skit. Mr. Hill helped students come up with ideas if they got stuck, but really put the pressure on them to develop these skits independently.

Behavioral Rehearsal and Feedback

The final activity around each skill was a performance of the social skit. The students performed the skit in front of a revolving panel that showed up right at 7:45 a.m. on

---

Skit Location (pick one):   Waiting for the bus   Friend's house   Lunchroom

Focus Skill: Initiations

Actor #1 (_____): Walks in and sees the other two characters standing and talking. Approaches and says "_____"

Actor #2 (_____): Turns when Actor 1 approaches. Waits for Actor 1 to speak. Then responds by _____

Actor #3 (_____): After Actor 2 responds to the initiation by Actor 1, adds to this interaction by _____

Then what? Decide together how to end this skit in a natural way. Write out lines as needed.

_____

_____

_____

_____

_____

Figure 2.7. Script stem that Mr. Hill designed to structure the students' skit.

Thursdays. This panel consisted of recruited "experts" and included other teachers, building administrators, university professors, and graduate students. These experts were given the evaluation materials (e.g., rubrics, visual scales) and rated the students' performances on these targeted skills. They also gave the students a more global rating related to intangible social skills that were untrained. These behavioral rehearsals were also videotaped for use in the guided problem-solving routines discussed earlier. The purpose of these expert panels was to mimic the high stakes of real-life social situations and attempt to put students into situations that felt like the encounters they experienced daily. Panel experts were primed by Mr. Hill to be kind but direct with regard to evaluation of the students' performances.

Culminating Experience

After Mr. Hill addressed each skill in the ways discussed here, he still had 2 weeks of the 10-week program. During these 2 weeks, Mr. Hill worked with the students to develop a short movie that demonstrated all the skills that they had worked on during the CBI program. The students were required to demonstrate all the skills addressed. The students then screened their movies and used the evaluation materials to rate their behavior across the different skills. The CBI program culminated with this screening.

While the program described in this case study took time to plan and design, it was accomplished by a classroom teacher with a full caseload and considerable daily responsibilities. Mr. Hill's case is an example of what can be accomplished when teachers understand CBI programs and can leverage these unique approaches to address complex social behaviors.

◯◯ Summary Considerations

In closing, we hope the material outlined in this guide will help classroom teachers and other practitioners develop and implement self-management, cognitive behavior, and related tools for students with ASD. We feel strongly that students with ASD can benefit greatly from methods that leverage both behavioral and cognitive approaches to improve outcomes. Beyond the effects of these tools on specific targeted skills, SMI and CBI also have the potential to help students with ASD become more self-aware, more self-regulated, and more self-determined. Improvements in these areas can positively impact postsecondary outcomes for students with ASD and add positively to their overall quality of life. Further, classroom teachers and other school personnel are likely to benefit greatly from these tools, as they have the capacity to be student managed and thereby increase teachers' capacity to engage in the important work of planning and implementing instruction.

Related to implementation of these tools, we again want to stress that these tools should be developed with individual students in mind and should be implemented systematically over time, and the effects of these tools should be closely monitored. We also emphasize the prerequisite skills identified for each of the tools, and we urge practitioners to select students that can best access and take advantage of the benefits of these methods.

⌗ References

Adrien, J. L., Martineau, J., Barthélémy, C., Bruneau, N., Garreau, B., & Sauvage, D. (1995). Disorders of regulation of cognitive activity in autistic children. *Journal of Autism and Developmental Disorders, 25*(3), 249–263.

Alberto, P. A., & Troutman, A. C. (2012). *Applied behavior analysis for teachers* (9th ed.). Upper Saddle River, NJ: Pearson

Barlow, J., Wright, C., Sheasby, J., Turner, A., & Hainsworth, J. (2002). Self-management approaches for people with chronic conditions: A review. *Patient Education and Counseling, 48*(2), 177–187.

Ben-Zeev, D., Kaiser, S. M., Brenner, C. J., Begale, M., Duffecy, J., & Mohr, D. C. (2013). Development and usability testing of FOCUS: A smartphone system for self-management of schizophrenia. *Psychiatric Rehabilitation Journal, 36*(4), 289.

Berkovits, L., Eisenhower, A., & Blacher, J. (2017). Emotion regulation in young children with autism spectrum disorders. *Journal of Autism and Developmental Disorders, 47*(1), 68–79.

Blair, C., & Diamond, A. (2008). Biological processes in prevention and intervention: The promotion of self-regulation as a means of preventing school failure. *Development and Psychopathology, 20*(3), 899–911.

Burke, L. E., Wang, J., & Sevick, M. A. (2011). Self-monitoring in weight loss: A systematic review of the literature. *Journal of the American Dietetic Association, 111*(1), 92–102.

Buron, K. D., & Curtis, M. (2003). *The incredible 5-point scale: Assisting students with ASD in understanding social interactions and controlling their emotional responses.* Shawnee Mission, KS: Autism Asperger.

Cooper, J. O., Heron, T. E., & Heward, W. L. (2007). *Applied behavior analysis* (2nd ed.). Upper Saddle River, NJ: Pearson Education.

Crutchfield, S. A., Mason, R. A., Chambers, A., Wills, H. P., & Mason, B. A. (2015). Use of a self-monitoring application to reduce stereotypic behavior in adolescents with autism: A preliminary investigation of I-Connect. *Journal of Autism and Developmental Disorders, 45*(5), 1146.

Crutchfield, S., Weber, S., & Simpson, R. L. (2014). A novel peer-based social skills instructional program for middle school learners with higher functioning autism. *Autism– Open Access, 4*, 1–5.

Davis, J. L., Mason, B. A., Davis, H. S., Mason, R. A., & Crutchfield, S. A. (2016). Self-monitoring interventions for students with ASD: A meta-analysis of school-based research. *Review Journal of Autism and Developmental Disorders, 3*(3), 196–208.

Deitchman, C., Reeve, S. A., Reeve, K. F., & Progar, P. R. (2010). Incorporating video feedback into self-management training to promote generalization of social initiations by children with autism. *Education and Treatment of Children, 33*(3), 475–488.

Hofmann, S. G., Asnaani, A., Vonk, I. J., Sawyer, A. T., & Fang, A. (2012). The efficacy of cognitive behavioral therapy: A review of meta-analyses. *Cognitive Therapy and Research, 36*(5), 427–440.

Jahromi, L. B., Bryce, C. I., & Swanson, J. (2013). The importance of self-regulation for the school and peer engagement of children with high-functioning autism. *Research in Autism Spectrum Disorders, 7*(2), 235–246.

Kim, J. A., Szatmari, P., Bryson, S. E., Streiner, D. L., & Wilson, F. J. (2000). The prevalence of anxiety and mood problems among children with autism and Asperger syndrome. *Autism, 4*(2), 117–132.

Kirschner, P. A., Sweller, J., & Clark, R. E. (2006). Why minimal guidance during instruction does not work: An analysis of the failure of constructivist, discovery, problem-based, experiential, and inquiry-based teaching. *Educational Psychologist, 41*(2), 75–86.

Koegel, R. L., & Koegel, L. K. (1990). Extended reductions in stereotypic behavior of students with autism through a self-management treatment package. *Journal of Applied Behavior Analysis, 23*(1), 119.

Koegel, R. L., Koegel, L. K., & McNerney, E. K. (2001). Pivotal areas in intervention for autism. *Journal of Clinical Child Psychology, 30*(1), 19–32.

Lacava, P. G., Golan, O., Baron-Cohen, S., & Smith Myles, B. (2007). Using assistive technology to teach emotion recognition to students with Asperger syndrome: A pilot study. *Remedial and Special Education, 28*(3), 174–181.

Laugeson, E. A., Frankel, F., Gantman, A., Dillon, A. R., & Mogil, C. (2012). Evidence-based social skills training for adolescents with autism spectrum disorders: The UCLA PEERS program. *Journal of autism and developmental disorders, 42*(6), 1025–1036.

Lee, S. H., Palmer, S. B., & Wehmeyer, M. L. (2009). Goal setting and self-monitoring for students with disabilities. *Intervention in School and Clinic, 44*, 139–145.

Lee, S. H., Simpson, R. L., & Shogren, K. A. (2007). Effects and implications of self-management for students with autism: A meta-analysis. *Focus on Autism and Other Developmental Disabilities, 22*(1), 2–13.

Liss, M., Fein, D., Allen, D., Dunn, M., Feinstein, C., Morris, R., . . . Rapin, I. (2001). Executive functioning in high-functioning children with autism. *Journal of Child Psychology and Psychiatry and Allied Disciplines, 42*(2), 261–270.

Loveland, K. A. (2005). Social-emotional impairment and self-regulation in autism spectrum disorders. In J. Nadel & D. Muir (Eds.), *Emotional development* (pp. 365–382). Oxford, UK: Oxford University Press.

Maag, J. W. (1989). Use of cognitive mediation strategies for social skills training: Theoretical and conceptual issues. *Monograph in Behavioral Disorders, 12*, 87–100.

Maione, L., & Mirenda, P. (2006). Effects of video modeling and video feedback on peer-directed social language skills of a child with autism. *Journal of Positive Behavior Interventions, 8*(2), 106–118.

McGee, G. G., Krantz, P. J., & McClannahan, L. E. (1984). Conversational skills for autistic adolescents: Teaching assertiveness in naturalistic game settings. *Journal of Autism and Developmental Disorders, 14*(3), 319–330.

Mennuti, R. B., Freeman, A., & Christner, R. W. (Eds.). (2006). *Cognitive-behavioral interventions in educational settings: A handbook for practice.* New York, NY: Routledge.

Muchmore, D. B., Springer, J., & Miller, M. (1994). Self-monitoring of blood glucose in overweight type 2 diabetic patients. *Acta diabetologica, 31*(4), 215–219.

National Autism Center. (2015). *Evidenced-based practice and autism in the schools* (2nd ed.). Randolph, MA: Author.

Newman, B., Buffington, D. M., & Hemmes, N. (1996). Self-reinforcement used to increase the appropriate conversation of autistic teenagers. *Education and Training in Mental Retardation and Developmental Disabilities, 31*, 304–309.

Nicklas, B. J., Gaukstern, J. E., Beavers, K. M., Newman, J. C., Leng, X., & Rejeski, W. J. (2014). Self-monitoring of spontaneous physical activity and sedentary behavior to prevent weight regain in older adults. *Obesity, 22*(6), 1406–1412.

Ozonoff, S., & McEvoy, R. E. (1994). A longitudinal study of executive function and theory of mind development in autism. *Development and Psychopathology, 6*(3), 415–431.

Pearson, P. D., & Gallagher, M. C. (1983). The instruction of reading comprehension. *Contemporary Educational Psychology, 8*, 317–344.

Quinn, C., Swaggart, B. L., & Myles, B. S. (1994). Implementing cognitive behavior management programs for persons with autism: Guidelines for practitioners. *Focus on Autistic Behavior, 9*(4), 1–13.

Reinecke, D. R., Newman, B., & Meinberg, D. L. (1999). Self-management of sharing in three pre-schoolers with autism. *Education and Training in Mental Retardation and Developmental Disabilities, 34*, 312–317.

Sands, D. J., & Doll, B. (2000). *Teaching goal setting and decision making to students with developmental disabilities.* Washington, DC: American Association on Intellectual and Developmental Disabilities.

Scarpa, A., White, S. W., & Attwood, T. (Eds.). (2013). *CBT for children and adolescents with high-functioning autism spectrum disorders.* New York, NY: Guilford Press.

Shogren, K. A., & Wehmeyer, M. L. (2018). *Self-determination* (PRO-ED series on autism spectrum disorders). Austin, TX: PRO-ED.

Shogren, K. A., Wehmeyer, M. L., Burke, K. M., & Palmer, S. B. (2017). *The self-determination learning model of instruction: Teacher's guide.* Lawrence, KS: Kansas University Center on Developmental Disabilities.

Simpson, R., & Crutchfield, S. (2013). Effective educational practices for children and youth with autism spectrum disorders: Issues, recommendations, and trends. In B. Cook, M. Tankersley, & T. J. Landrum (Eds.), *Evidence-based practices* (pp. 197–220). Bingley, UK: Emerald Group.

Simpson, R. L., & Myles, B. S. (Eds.). (2008). *Educating children and youth with autism: Strategies for effective practice.* Austin, TX: PRO-ED.

Stahmer, A. C., & Schreibman, L. (1992). Teaching children with autism appropriate play in unsupervised environments using a self-management treatment package. *Journal of Applied Behavior Analysis, 25*, 447–459.

Stichter, J. P., & Conroy, M. A. (2018). *Social skills and social interactions* (PRO-ED series on autism spectrum disorders). Austin, TX: PRO-ED.

Thiemann, K. S., & Goldstein, H. (2001). Social stories, written text cues, and video feedback: Effects on social communication of children with autism. *Journal of Applied Behavior Analysis, 34*(4), 425–446.

Tobin, C. E., & Simpson, R. (2012). Consequence maps: A novel behavior management tool for educators. *Teaching Exceptional Children, 44*(5), 68–75.

White, S. W., Ollendick, T., Albano, A. M., Oswald, D., Johnson, C., Southam-Gerow, M. A., . . . Scahill, L. (2013). Randomized controlled trial: Multimodal anxiety and social skill intervention for adolescents with autism spectrum disorder. *Journal of Autism and Developmental Disorders, 43*(2), 382–294.

Wilkinson, L. A. (2008). Self-management for children with high-functioning autism spectrum disorders. *Intervention in School and Clinic, 43*(3), 150–157.

Winner, M. G. (2005). *Think social!: A social thinking curriculum for school-age students: For teaching social thinking and related social skills to students with high functioning autism, Asperger syndrome, PDD-NOS, ADHD, nonverbal learning disability and for all others in the murky gray area of social thinking.* Santa Clara, CA: Think Social.

Yeung, A. S., & Yeung, A. S. (2016). Self-management for autism spectrum disorders: A review. *North American Journal of Medicine and Science, 8*(3), 123–128.

Zirpoli, T. J. (2008). *Behavior management: Applications for teachers* (5th ed.). Upper Saddle River, NJ: Prentice Hall.

About the Editor and Authors

Richard L. Simpson was professor emeritus, University of Kansas. During his more than 40 years as a professor of special education at the University of Kansas, he directed numerous demonstration programs for students with autism spectrum disorder (ASD) and other disabilities and coordinated a variety of federal grant programs related to students with ASD and other disabilities. He also worked as a teacher of students with disabilities, a psychologist, and an administrator of programs for students with autism. He was the former editor of the professional journal *Focus on Autism and Other Developmental Disabilities* (published by the Hammill Institute on Disabilities) and the author of numerous books and articles on ASD.

Stephen A. Crutchfield, PhD, is an assistant professor of special education at California Polytechnic State University. Dr. Crutchfield earned his doctorate from the University of Kansas in 2014, with an emphasis in ASD. As a classroom teacher, Dr. Crutchfield taught students with ASD in both middle school and elementary school settings for 5 years. In his own research, Dr. Crutchfield is examining technology-delivered self-monitoring systems and automated, eco-behavioral measurement systems for learners with ASD and other developmental disabilities.

Leah Wood, PhD, BCBA-D, is an assistant professor of special education at California Polytechnic State University. Dr. Wood earned her doctorate from the University of North Carolina at Charlotte in 2014 in special education, with an emphasis on moderate and severe disabilities. She is also a Board Certified Behavior Analyst (BCBA-D). As a classroom teacher, Dr. Wood taught students with mild to severe intellectual disability for 6 years. In her own research, Dr. Wood is examining academic interventions for students with developmental disabilities, both with and without the application of technology. Specifically, she develops interventions intended to promote comprehension of text across content and formats and the acquisition of science practices.